Miracles of Courage

Miracles of Courage

HOW FAMILIES MEET
THE CHALLENGE OF A CHILD'S
CRITICAL ILLNESS

MONICA DICKENS

Introduction by Dr. John Truman,
Chief of the Pediatric Hematology/Oncology Unit,
Massachusetts General Hospital

DODD, MEAD & COMPANY NEW YORK

Published by Dodd, Mead & Company, Inc.
79 Madison Avenue, New York, N.Y. 10016
Distributed in Canada by
McClelland and Stewart Limited, Toronto
Manufactured in the United States of America

Designed by G. G. Laurens

First Edition

Library of Congress Cataloging in Publication Data

Dickens, Monica, 1915–
    Miracles of courage.

    1. Terminally ill children—Family relationships.
2. Chronically ill children—Family relationships.
3. Courage. I. Title.
RJ249.D53   1985   362.1'989299419   84-28717
ISBN 0-396-08554-7

To everyone who has helped me
to write this book:
the families, the children, and those who work
with them.
My love and thanks.

Introduction 🌿

*T*his is a book of praise and celebration. It honors the bravery, endurance, and good humor that mankind is capable of summoning in the face of adversity. It honors children who are stricken by dread diseases and dreadful treatments, but who continue in school and continue to love life. It honors parents who rise to heroic stature in seeing that their children receive every medical advantage and every measure of loving support as they make their journey.

For those of us who are lucky enough to work with these families, it is a constantly humbling and renewing experience. No day passes that a lump does not come to my throat nor a tear to my eye. Can you imagine my emotions as I stand ready to give a long spinal needle to a sixteen-year-old who has given me a plate of brownies? Or, having just finished a painful bone marrow test on a three-year-old, I am given a big kiss? Can you imagine telling a young couple that their only child has leukemia and then receiving their thanks for being the bearer of such news? People are truly remarkable in their ability to rise to any challenge, and overwhelming in their capacity for mutual love. Remove the veneer that makes people appear so different and you find a fathomless treasure of goodness. After twenty years of working with children who have cancer, I am a confirmed optimist, convinced that good outweighs evil in the bosom of mankind and that good will ultimately triumph in the march of human affairs.

This book also honors science. I view science as the ultimate achievement of the human intellect, and science has responded nobly to the plight of children with cancer. When I started to work in this field in the early '60s few children could be cured. Now, more than half will outlive me. Science has made such progress through the meticulous work of many laboratory workers who bring new drugs and techniques to clinical investigators for trial. It is a slow process and often requires some children to be treated one way and others differently so that a new idea can be compared with the old. To some extent this requires gambling with fate, yet I am always amazed at how eager parents and even children are to strike out in new directions.

Life, in all its complexity of meaning, is a beautiful experience, and the potential of the human soul is infinite. Any who doubt this I invite to meet the families described in this book.

John T. Truman, M.D.
Massachusetts General Hospital

Miracles of Courage

Chapter ONE 🌿

*T*his is a story about survival, and the triumph of the human spirit.

It is a celebration of the parents and families of desperately sick children, who once hoped, like the rest of us, that those kinds of things only happened to other people.

Knocked down by terrible random blows of disaster, they struggle up again and start to plod on, day after day, doing what has to be done. They get angry and resentful and confused and devastated. But I have seen how they perform miracles of love and endurance and how they turn the disaster into a power of the spirit that they might not have found if disaster had let them alone.

"People tell me I'm strong." The mother of a child with leukemia sits patiently in the waiting room of the hospital clinic waiting for test results. "I'm not. You just do as much as you can. What else is there to do?"

"One day at a time?"

She smiles at my innocence. "One hour, more like."

This waiting room at Massachusetts General Hospital in Boston is always moderately chaotic, with dolls and toy cars flung about, small chairs overturned, and paper shredded on the carpet, not surprisingly, since it is shared by several children's clinics. One of them is Dr. John Truman's clinic for children who have cancer and various blood diseases.

Across from the patient mother, a grandmother reads to a child on her lap, who may be a boy or a girl, with a narrow bald head and huge dark glasses, like an insect from space.

A middle-aged woman in a white coat talks candidly to an attentive black girl who has colored beads dangling from myriad tiny braids. They both suddenly break into laughter, and the older woman slaps the younger one on the lean thigh of her jeans and says quite loudly, "Oh, I don't worry about you!"

A small boy whose chemotherapy has left him only a few bleached wisps of hair goes up and down the miniature slide over and over, solemnly, as if it were work. His parents watch him, also solemnly, their faces blank with anxiety, not talking to each other.

A healthy older girl hurls hollow blocks at people's legs and knocks other children away from the blackboard, oblivious to "Stop that, Jennifer!" from a tired mother with another pushy child and a baby asleep in a frayed denim sling on her ruined bosom.

A door opening brings the sound of a child crying, but another child is laughing with a grown-up, and there is a short, amateurish burst of harmonica music. A young woman comes through from the hematology clinic, and the solemn parents smile and stand up. The little boy comes down the slide and runs to grab the young woman around the legs.

"Come on through. Dr. Truman will be back soon, and we don't want to keep you waiting out here. I just got the blood counts. They look good."

She gives the child her hand, and the parents take each other's hands and follow.

This book is about parents like these who, with their children, fight such life-threatening diseases as leukemia, Hodgkin's disease, osteosarcoma, and the lethal anemias. I got to know them after my daughter became one of them, a hospital mother: one of the secret, unknown band of titans in an underworld in which most of us, thank God, never have to live.

My daughter Pamela, small and still childish looking, optimistic, unacquainted with tragedy, was hurled unprepared into the deadly illness of her small twin son, and I watched the giant effort with which she grew brave and strong because of it.

My two daughters are adopted. After Pam had been married for a while, she wanted to have a baby. Nothing happened, so she and Bob went to a doctor, whose clumsy advice was "Why not adopt? You can always get a Vietnamese baby," missing the point that because she was adopted herself, with no known ancestors, Pam was particularly anxious to start her own dynasty.

He also missed what was wrong with her. When her unexplained blackouts were eventually traced to hypoglycemia and treated, she doubled her expectations by having twin boys.

"Oh, lookit the twins!"

When Pam and I propelled them through the indoor shopping mall the next winter in a tandem stroller, every other woman veered toward us with a dotty smile and delighted eyebrows.

"Twins!" They wagged their heads knowingly at the boys. "Double trouble," three women out of four told us. Pam made her blank face, because why could they not see that it was double joy? We were now so used to having two babies, that we did not see how anybody could possibly make do with only one.

But when Jim and Steve were almost a year old, the bottom dropped out of our cozy world, and we were in danger of finding out.

One Sunday night, Steve woke with a rash everywhere on his body—top of head, palms of hands, soles of feet. He was burning with fever. The man who was on call for their doctor mumbled sleepily, not interested.

"His temperature's a hundred and four."

"Uh-huh."

"Well, I—" Pam reddened, as if he were in the same room.

"Babies often go that high."

"He's not well. He looks terrible. He has a rash all over."

"Take him to your own doctor tomorrow."

"Can't you see him now?"

"Look—I've already been called out of bed to the hospital twice tonight. Don't fuss. A hundred and four isn't the end of the world."

Pam was going to cry, and Bob snatched the phone from her. He lost his temper and shouted overwrought, soap-opera things like "Dammit, this is my son!" and the doctor sighed and agreed to meet them in the emergency room.

Quite angry, he refused to speak to Bob, except to grunt that he didn't appreciate being yelled at by hysterical parents when he had just got to bed at three A.M. He told Pam to take the child home to a mild aspirin dose and a cool bath.

"Some kind of virus. Don't worry."

It was a virus, but of a vicious and malevolent nature not guessed at by that tired doctor. In the next few days, Steve began to moan like a woman with menstrual cramps. His temperature shot up, his rash was a brilliant sunburned red, and he was admitted to the local hospital. When his temperature rose to a hundred and five and he seemed to be dying, he was taken to Children's Hospital in Boston.

In this excellent hospital, I found Pam sitting on a hard chair in a tiny isolation room, the naked baby clinging to the front of her like a fetus worn outside. The rash on his back was inflamed into raised sores. The skin of his face was breaking down like third-degree burns. His closed eyes were crusted and suppurating. The constant moaning cry was hoarse and ragged, from a throat raw with thrush. The hand that connected him to the intravenous drip, wrapped in a boxing glove of bandages with half a paper

4

cup over the needle, hung helplessly down on the splint. His head lolled backward on his crumpled scarlet neck. In a corner of the room, a pile of wet diapers waited for collection, and two cockroaches sojourned along the wall among the crumbs of Pam and Bob's sandwiches.

When the baby's fingertips and toes began to peel, the rare virus disease was positively identified as Kawasaki, named not for the motorcycle but for the Japanese doctor who identified this virulent set of symptoms.

The treatment was high doses of aspirin, and blood and cardiac monitoring, because of the raised sedimentation rate and the loss of white cells. Kawasaki complications are clotting, aneurysm, heart damage, tissue scarring, and loss of defense against other infections; also possible brain damage from the high fever—if the child lives.

Pam held the baby continuously, day and night. If she went for a meal or a shower, he screamed hoarsely and unstoppably, pulling himself up to the cot bars with a desperate strength.

On my first visit, I was too shocked by what was happening in Steve's room to notice much about the hospital. The next time, he was asleep with his raw face on the mattress and his raw bottom in the air; Pam fell asleep in the chair, so I explored and began to talk to other parents.

You could guess by a mother's appearance how long her child had been here. A distraught and anxious woman with a fairly smooth face was probably in the first crisis. Those who had been here longer, abandoning families to manage somehow, for the needs of the sick child, looked older than their years, dragged down, enduring.

In the cafeteria, two South American parents sat and waited, not much to say to each other, no English to speak to anyone else, while staff and patients and children on crutches and preoccupied women in white coats with pockets full of notes brought food to the table and ate their lunches and left.

I had clam chowder with a father whose infant son had

5

died upstairs an hour before. His wife was not ready to leave the baby.

"I couldn't stay in that room any longer," the young man said. He had a broad, mild face, with sandy eyelashes and a pink mouth under a soft moustache. "I've spent too much time in there, too many nights in that chair. And I've said . . . well, what you *do* say, before he"—he was going to say "died" but perhaps remembered, now that the crude actuality of dying was over, that he had been taught to say more primly—"passed on. In case he could hear me. You hear about that, don't you—people hearing, even when they're in a coma? Then after, when they had wrapped him in a blanket, I was suddenly terribly hungry. Isn't that weird?"

At last Pam was able to bring Steven home, with one of his lives squandered, his head half shaved for the in-travenous needles, still sick and skinny and dull of eye—but alive and cured, with no apparent after-effects. Pam was no longer a hospital mother, but I found myself still passionately interested in those who were.

I had heard that there was a children's doctor at Massachusetts General Hospital who was particularly involved with the families of very sick children.

"If you want to know about parents," I was told, "go to John Truman. He probably knows more about them than anyone."

I was afraid I might be a nuisance, but I was welcomed with the same warmth and reassurance the staff gives the patients, and Dr. Truman agreed to let me follow the work of the clinic and the wards and talk with his children and teenagers and their parents, both past and present. So for about two years, I have enhanced my life by getting to know these families, both at the hospital and in their homes and mine.

In the hospital I always get a nostalgic sense of belonging. I feel once more a part of this urgent, purposeful world

6

to which I used to belong when I was a nurse in London. At Mass. General, I am an observer now, not a doer. I am only a ghost here, a hanger-on; yet I have some small function as a listener, a chronicler. And perhaps someone has to be that, so that the pain, the unnoticeable heroism, the committed intelligence of a doctor, the exactness of a researcher, the day-by-day repetitive motions of a nurse will not go unrecorded.

What some of the children have to go through is undeserved, terrifying, exhausting, and far beyond what most people have to endure in a lifetime. What many of the parents go through is indescribable, but the attempt to describe it is why I am here, a watcher and a listener. What happens to these people? How do they grapple with calamities that the rest of us, who have not yet been tested to the limit, know would break us?

How do ordinary people become giants? The mothers, who have been dealt so many blows and reeled back for more, seem to me in some way ennobled. Not by the pain itself; I don't believe you have to suffer to become worthwhile. But by what they have done with the pain.

With their eyes set in bruised shadows and the new fine lines on the young faces that are there now forever, and their candid, unassuming voices, they are supremely approachable. They have shed reticence along with the security torn from them at the moment of diagnosis. Yet they seem above my reach, somehow magical.

What is it about them that attracts me so and pulls me back to hear story after story? Not curiosity. I need to be with them. I need to hear them talk. Not a morbid attraction to pain; I am drawn to the magnet of their strength.

Is it the ordeal that makes the parents remarkable? They can't answer that, because they don't see themselves as I do. They are pleased with what they are doing, but not impressed. I may see them as ennobled, but they have to manage without the aid of glory.

Despair? A breakdown? That's a luxury only someone

7

with less reason can afford. They do what has to be done, day by day, month by month, because there is nothing else to do. There are no choices of how to behave. This is what you do.

Massachusetts General, the teaching hospital for Harvard Medical School, is the oldest hospital in New England. It took in its first patient in 1821 and made history in 1846 when the first use of ether in surgery was publicly demonstrated on a young printer in the amphitheater under architect Charles Bulfinch's great dome, known ever since as the Ether Dome.

It is a huge rambling old hospital, part clean and modern, part shabby and archaic, which treats and researches almost every ailment of the body and mind. Over the years, many buildings of different periods and styles have been crowded around the original Bulfinch building between the gentle Charles River and the clamorous modern edifices of Government Center.

Dr. John Truman's pediatric hematology clinic on the sixth floor of a trim new outpatient building might be part of any modern hospital, until you look down from the windows to the enduring reminder of the gray pillared portico and dome of the old Bulfinch building.

Most of the children who have to spend so much of their young lives at this clinic have some form of cancer. About two thirds have leukemia, and one third have solid tumors, or Hodgkin's disease, which is cancer of the lymphatic system. The other blood diseases treated here don't need such frequent hospital visits, and unless the child lives in Boston, will usually be followed up in continuing treatment at a local hospital.

On my first visit, I sat with the clinic staff at their early-morning discussion of the fifteen children and adolescents they were to see that day for tests and treatment. Dr. Truman, who has no self-importance, was the one who collected extra chairs. With each patient, he talked about the family and what was going on. He smiled when he spoke of the tremendous efforts made by parents and used the words, quite casually, but with conviction, *nobility of spirit,* and I knew I had come to the right place to find what I was looking for.

Come there with me. Come to the Oncology Unit of the Pediatric Hematology Department in the Ambulatory Care Building of Massachusetts General Hospital. The pedantic orotundity of its name is just a front. It is a place that, in spite of the sights it has to see and the stories it has to hear and the pain it must inflict by the necessary intrusion of needles into the veins, spinal columns, and bone marrow of undeserving children, can be described as rather cozy.

The general waiting room is shared by several clinics: Endocrinology, Hematology, and Learning Disorders. The staff tries not to make parents and their children wait out there if they can possibly find room for them inside the clinic. Not only because a child from another clinic might bring a risk of an infection to a child on chemotherapy, which impairs the body's defenses, but also because these are anxious families who are more comfortable, even squeezed into a corner, if they can feel part of what's going on in the clinic.

Once out of the waiting room and through the glass door, it is all smiling recognition and cries of welcome and pleasure, as if you were the sole reason for them all coming to work that day. Even I, with no child in tow, trying not to get in the way, afraid I might be intruding here once too often, am greeted eagerly, as if I were a bonus, rather than the nuisance that anyone must be who is trying to find out what is going on in a place where everyone is busy seeing that it does go on.

On some of the tapes I made talking with parents in a side room during the hours it takes for their children to get the drugs intravenously, the background noises suggest the rich flavor of Pediatric Hematology. There are some heartrending shrieks of rage from a little boy who doesn't have any more good veins to get a needle into, and a babble of Italian from parents and uncles and cousins who come en masse to help a four-year-old have a blood transfusion. Then more tears and a brief bellow of "I wanna go home!" But there are also cherishing sounds of commiseration, laughter, and friendly voices calling back and forth, music from the radio a young patient has brought to ease the tedium of chemotherapy, a bit of *Mary Poppins* from the videotape player, and exclamations of approval and pleasure from the clinic staff.

"My other son was ten at the time." Judy's comfortable voice is running on the tape. *"Some kids at the school said to him, 'Your brother has leukemia. How come he isn't dead?' "*

Behind her voice, there is a burst of sound as a door opens and someone is welcomed with cries of loving joy, like a family reunion.

"He lost his hair when he was five, from the chemotherapy, and people were terrible. Just to take him to the supermarket and take his hat off—everybody stared at him. A woman followed us around the store."

"Oh! You brought cake. Come on, everybody, into Dr. Truman's office. It's teatime."

"Even coming into the hospital"—the background noises are not incongruous to her; her voice widens and goes upward with a smile in it—*"people would turn and look at us. You'd think they'd know in a place like this. But people are funny. We don't let it bother us, do we, Christopher?"*

The fainter voice of her son, now twelve, with hair grown in spikily, who is on a bed with the Adriamycin running into his outstretched hand, listening solemnly to her recital of his story, adds, *"If you say so, Ma."*

The door of our room opens. *"Gingerbread, anyone?"*

The people at the center of this lively warmth, which does not camouflage the life-and-death business of the clinic but makes it at least more bearable for those who have to be here, are Dr. Truman's long-time nurse Monica; Sue, his nurse-clinician; and Cindy, his secretary. Coming and going among them are other doctors and residents, medical students, nurses who come from the ward to give continuity for small patients, and various "fellows" doing special training in hematology, like easygoing Bill, and Elizabeth, a young doctor with waterfall hair and a gentle nineteenth-century air of having a fluid spine.

Monica, a quiet-voiced and perfectly charming woman, has been Dr. Truman's nurse for thirty years and is called Gramma Monica by some of the younger children.

Sue is fair, with a bright color and the kind of softly smiling face you'd prefer to have bending over you if something painful has to be done. As a nurse-practitioner, she does physicals as well as the test and treatment procedures, and also some teaching for the nurses at the hospital.

"Sue?" parents say when you ask them about her, and then they smile and sigh. "Oh, *Sue.*"

Cindy, who has been Dr. Truman's secretary for eight years, is firmly attached to the clinic "because this is the only job where I'm not treated like a dumb blond secretary." She knows everything about all the patients, and their parents will sometimes talk to her freely because she isn't a doctor or a nurse. If you don't find her in her office, she'll be playing on the floor with a small child or sitting with someone in the waiting room or one of the treatment rooms, keeping up their morale.

Cindy is often used as a lure by mothers of small children in stubborn fear of a trip to the clinic. "Want to go and see Cindy?"

"Okay."

"Want to go and see Cindy and Sue and Monica and Dr. Truman?" The mother of a small anemic girl who remained cheerful even when her bone marrow had virtually shut down as a blood cell factory always got the answer, "Just what I wanted to do today."

These skilled, solicitous people work together very closely

and share with each other things they can't discuss with family or friends: fears, losses, disappointments. Outside people are too ready to pounce on anything negative that reinforces their ideas about cancer. If you are doing important work that you love, you don't want to be asked, "How do you do this day after day?"

John Truman, who runs this emporium for leukemia, sarcoma, Hodgkin's disease, hemophilia, sickle-cell and aplastic anemias, and other blood diseases, is a remarkable man of brilliance and compassion, like many of the best doctors in his field.

He is tall, slender, pale, and rather delicate looking, in his late forties but deceptively boyish. Early in the morning, coming clear-eyed and hopeful to the day, he sometimes looks like a teenager with graying hair.

He has a gentle voice and a way of considering before answering questions that can be more convincing than when a brisk-witted person comes instantly back at you. He is, of course, nimble enough to shoot you a quick, intelligent answer, but in the pause, you feel that he prefers to polish off the edges a bit, to consider the questioner as well as the question, to make sure you get the kind of answer you need.

This careful way of answering questions must be reassuring to patients and their families. He does generate trust, they tell me. He has to. You can't go doubting into something as devastating as cancer treatment.

Although he can help parents to make informed decisions, a lot of the time they must accept the treatment plan because he and other specialists believe it to be the best there is, for this child, at this time.

Thirty-five years ago, a child with acute lymphocytic leukemia had about three months to live. Now, depending on age, general health, and many variables, the treatment offers a fifty to ninety-five percent chance of remission. The longer the remission lasts after the drugs are stopped, the greater the confidence with which it can be called a cure.

For the children at the low end of the percentages, whose remissions come not at all or only temporarily and are each time shorter and harder to achieve, the doctor is still the focal point of trust.

He must always be there for the people who have to depend on him, solidly rooted in his knowledge and experience. They need to know that he is available. They need to know that they can call him, even if they don't call him.

When Dr. Truman was in general practice with children, there would always be about four calls a night from anxious mothers, usually with trivial problems. Now that his mothers are coping with cancer, he may answer the telephone once every third evening that he is on call and be woken only once a month in the middle of the night.

He has formulated Truman's Aphorism: "There is an inverse relationship between the severity of the illness and the number of times the physician is called."

Families of very sick children know more and have more experience and confidence. But they have Dr. Truman's home number, and often it is enough just to know that they can call him at any time.

One night when three-year-old David had croup and his harsh breathing frightened his mother Deborah, she called the doctor after midnight.

"I'm sorry to bother you."

"Don't worry. I was just sitting here reading a book," he said cheerfully, although Deborah was sure he was lying, since she knew he was in the hospital every morning by eight o'clock.

Chapter T W O 🌿

*D*eborah was one of the first of the mothers I went to see at home. Her son David is now thirteen and perfectly well. He only goes to the clinic about once a year for routine tests, although Dr. Truman asks Deborah to come in at other times to help new parents to cope with the first stages of their child's leukemia and to use herself and her strong, healthy son as a promise that you can go through hell and come out as a survivor.

It was eleven years ago that David's illness began, as it does for many children, with a persistent cold. He was a cheerful, easy two-year-old, rather pale, his legs a bit bruised. He fell about a lot and his stomach was a bit swollen— but don't all stomachs stick out at that age? Deborah would not have taken him to her local doctor if she had not had an appointment for her new baby.

She did not worry when he said he wanted to do blood tests. That must be routine. But when he called her after she got home, she was surprised. Doctors don't call you. You usually have to call them for test results.

"The blood count is erratic. Get your husband from work and take David to Massachusetts General in Boston. Go to the Emergency Room. I've arranged for him to see Dr. Truman."

David had several symptoms, and his doctor was fairly sure, but many local doctors who are the first to see a leukemia child can't be sure or don't even suspect leukemia. That may be the doctor's fault or it may not, but a lot of the parents are resentful and angry afterward with their local pediatrician who, like Pam's tired doctor who had never seen a case of Kawasaki, had told them, "Take him home and give him an aspirin."

Whether the anger is justified or not, it at least gives them someone to rage at, since it is no use being angry with the cancer cells that have invaded their child's blood.

Mary's doctor did know that her tiny baby had leukemia, and he knew that, at two months old, the child didn't have much of a chance.

To Mary and Michael, a pair of very young waifs, both pale and thin with light red hair, he said kindly enough, "You can have other children."

But Mary and Michael, young and terrified as they were, fired up at him: "We want this one."

Sometimes the child has almost no symptoms and only is taken to the doctor because it is time for a regular checkup. Sometimes something like suspected tonsilitis is the reason for the blood test that turns up something much worse.

A teenager's increasing leg pains are thought to be muscle strain, because he's running or playing tennis or football—or is trying to as the pain gets worse.

Chris remembers, "It felt as if my legs were being expanded, but with no room to expand." A pretty accurate description, since what was happening was that the rampant abnormal white cells were crowding the marrow spaces of the bones.

The pediatrician may not have used the words *cancer* or *leukemia,* but may have said something like, "a significant blood disease." But because parents can see symptoms like bruising and fatigue, and now they find themselves being referred to a blood specialist, most of them suspect what is wrong, even though they may not admit it to themselves or each other until the diagnosis is spoken.

"I just knew," Alice said. "Driving into Boston, my husband kept saying, 'It could be this, it could be that,' but I had known as soon as our doctor told us to go to the hospital that it was leukemia. I just knew, but I thought if I didn't say anything, it wouldn't be true."

Even when it isn't leukemia, about half the parents think it is, giving Dr. Truman the unusual joy of bringing good news for a change to the people who are sent to him.

When the local doctor suspects or confirms leukemia from the blood tests and other signs like an enlarged spleen, the next step is swift. The parents are almost always sent immediately to a big city hospital or to one of the main cancer centers like the Sidney Farber Clinic at Children's Hospital in Boston or Mass. General, both of which treat children not only from all over New England but from all over the world.

In 1972, when Deborah and her husband rushed into Boston with David, much less was known about leukemia and its treatment than is known today. Dr. Truman's prognosis at that time was devastating.

"He has a fifty-fifty chance."

Deborah stared at him. *Chance—what does that mean? You take a child to the doctor to be cured, not to gamble with odds.*

Beside her on the bench, her husband put his hand on her arm, but she did not look at him. Somewhere down the hospital corridor, a child was screaming. David? Her special child, her tender, shining child who never cried?

"What did you say?" She had heard and not heard.

"Do you understand what's wrong with David?"

"No."

"Well." The doctor folded his long, deft fingers on the desk. "He does, in fact, have leukemia."

"What does that mean?"

"Cancer of the blood."

"Oh."

Their young married life had been holding together very serenely: a bright, attractive couple with a two-year-old and a small baby, and an income and a house and ideals about what love can do. Then without warning, the bottom dropped out.

"He has acute lymphocytic leukemia, but we know how to treat it. He'll be in this hospital at least a month."

The panicked thoughts, scurrying to find an escape: *We can't . . . we hadn't planned . . . he's never . . . you can't have him. . . . I have to take him home and pick up my baby.*

Deborah turned to her husband. He was crying, with difficulty, his face suffused and red, agonized.

"If David gets through this first month," the doctor said, "we'll go into three years of treatment. But he's very sick. He may not make it through the month."

Deborah was overwhelmed with weeping. The tall young doctor got up rather stiffly. He stood and looked down at them for a moment, still holding his fingers, started to say something, then just nodded and left them alone in the tiny windowless room, the terrible, impersonal, cruel room, a suffocating cradle of pain.

Later, when Dr. Truman came back into the little room, more brisk and businesslike, he explained the treatment and recited for them the foreign language of the drugs.

"It's all a blur now," he told Deborah's blank, devastated face, "but soon these names will roll off your tongue like everyday words." He told them that if they had brought David in a week ago, it would have been too soon to diagnose, but a week later, because of the speed with which leukemia cells multiply, he would have been dead within twenty-four hours.

After the blood transfusion, after her special, shining little boy, already shrunken with illness, feverish from crying, was asleep with needles and tubes in him, Deborah went home very late with Dave. They tried to look up leukemia in the dictionary, but they couldn't find it under *Lu.*

"If he survives this month, he has a fifty-fifty chance of recovery," Dr. Truman said. "Which fifty will you see? You can look at a bottle as half empty, or you can look at it as half full."

*   *   *

That was over ten years ago, when less was known about predicting the chances of leukemia patients. In 1985, thanks partly to pioneer patients like David, it is possible to say that a child newly diagnosed with acute lymphocytic leukemia has a ninety-five percent chance of an early remission.

It's what happens after this that makes the difference between success and failure.

Taking all ages and factors together, and all different types and courses of the disease, the overall leukemia prediction is a fifty-percent chance of a permanent cancer-free remission that may even be called a cure.

And parents are still going through what Deborah and Dave went through in the little impersonal room, still experiencing that suspended moment when their life was all right before, but is now suddenly shattered; still finding ways to pick the family out of the wreckage and survive.

The families remember precisely where and when they heard the diagnosis, and exactly what was said.

The mother of a little boy with a kidney tumor will never forget the tone of voice in which the surgeon said quite bluntly, "Neuroblastoma."

"Oh?" She looked up politely, not knowing what that meant.

"It gives him a fifty-fifty chance."

"Of dying?"

"But some of us do survive." He tried a smile on her then, realizing that he had broken the news badly. "Don't be afraid of the surgery." He stood up and pulled out his shirt and lifted it up to show her his own abdominal scar from God knew what.

Joe, the father of a splendid, strong young fifteen-year-old called J.B., had some out-of-date ideas about the treatment for leukemia and thought the diagnosis meant that the percentage of hope was zero.

"At J.B.'s age," Dr. Truman said, "he has a fifty-one percent chance."

Joe's first wife had died of cancer five years before. He had seen her suffer through chemotherapy and so he asked, "What about the side effects? Is it worth it?" and even J.B. said, "I don't want to do it if it's going to be worse than the illness."

Dr. Truman said, "Look—you're fifteen. The average normal lifespan for a male is sixty-six years. We're going for all of them."

Joe remembers the words exactly. "It was the turning point for us both toward saying, 'We can fight it.' "

Everyone remembers very clearly what they did with the news. What *can* you do? How can you receive that kind of news? A lifetime of experience would not prepare you.

One Italian mother let out a primeval scream that could be heard three floors below and fell off her chair in a swoon. Her husband, also Italian, sat and looked at her doubtfully, large tears following each other down his dropped cheeks. She lay for a moment as if dead, then rose up, got back on her chair, pulled down her skirt and said, "So okay. What do we do now?"

Laura was going to faint when the doctor told her that Krissie's "pulled muscle" from road races and ballet rehearsals was bone cancer. She was sitting on an examining table with her arm around Krissie, and as the blood dropped from her head into her stomach and she was pitching forward, a last reeling thought was, *Don't . . . pass . . . out.* She took a deep breath and was able to put her other arm around her trembling daughter and take the tremendous leap into the life that would be theirs now for weeks and months by starting to ask the questions. "What do we do first? What will happen? Then what will we do?"

But there is a lump in the way that makes it difficult to talk. A lump in the throat is not just a metaphor. It is actually there and can stay a long time, making it hard to talk, eat, and breathe. It is a strangling thing that prevents emotions from getting out, and any enjoyment from getting in.

If you don't break down at all, it may be because you have not yet taken it in.

When Brendan's mother heard, with only the surface of her hearing, the words *malignant tumor,* she went on smiling as if she had won the lottery. The doctors and nurses watched her to see when it would register. A student social worker who was there to learn about family reactions suggested, "It's all right to cry."

But she didn't until, in the car driving home to make arrangements for the other children so she could come back to the hospital, she suddenly began to howl like a dog.

Stacey felt that she was in a movie. "My husband had his head back against the wall, eyes staring. I was looking at Dr. Truman and crying feebly. I hadn't eaten for a week. It was all quite unreal, as if the doctor were saying lines of dialog written by somebody else, and we were all acting parts, and I was watching all of us from outside."

Calmness may be because you do hear and take in exactly what is said, but your instant self-protective reaction is *He's lying.* It is not until the doctor begins to talk about treatment and the percentages of hope that you can allow yourself to begin to believe it.

"Parents usually don't deny the truth of it," Dr. Truman says. "That's an adult mechanism people use for dealing with a cancer diagnosis for themselves. But as a parent, even though they're bowled over, they quite soon start to think clearly. Amazingly stoic they are, because they've got to keep strong, because of the child. They think of the child, not themselves."

Sometimes anger may be a shield against the diagnosis, as necessary as the anger at the initial physician who thought at first it was strep throat, mononucleosis, gastric flu—any of the things that are more likely for a child than cancer.

Marion is still angry with the first doctor, who thought her daughter Carol's tumor in the leg bone was a sprain or arthritis or a lesion.

"Stop worrying" was his bluff response. "You've always been too much of a worrier."

And four more days were wasted because the orthopedic surgeon was away.

When they saw the surgeon and heard him say, "Definitely a tumor, and it probably won't be good," Marion felt as if her life were being drained out of her. She looked at the young resident who was with the surgeon. He looked helplessly at her, and a little of her energy returned in an urge to comfort him, because he looked so upset, and so very young.

Then anger came, illogical but natural, against the surgeon who had broken the news.

What a terrible man, saying these cruel things so bluntly. Sixty-forty chance, he says, but what good is that? I want ninety-nine to one.

She left his office numb and stiff, shuffling, because her knees would not bend. Far ahead of her, unknowing, Carol walked jauntily down the corridor to the ward, a neat, spirited little girl with long blond hair bouncing down her back.

Some mothers talk about having felt relief, because the diagnosis was not as bad as they had feared. Sally brought her pale, feverish child from Spain. She had already made one trip from Madrid to Mass. General six months before and had gone home after none of the tests showed any leukemic cells. Now she was back, and Katie was so weak and ill that Sally was convinced she had aplastic anemia and would die unless she could have a last-chance bone marrow transplant.

When Dr. Truman said regretfully, "I'm afraid it *is* leukemia," Sally surprised him by answering briskly, "All right. Now we know where we are. Let's get on with the treatment. No mucking about."

Ann kept crying all the way to the hospital. "I cried at every corner we turned, every landmark that brought us closer, getting out of the car, walking into the hospital. My pediatrician hadn't said leukemia, but he hadn't joked with us, like he always did, and I knew. I'd known a girl my age who died of leukemia when I was thirteen, and I thought leukemia meant you would die.

"When Dr. Truman told us, he was very gentle, very positive, and I heard the word *hope* for the first time. My husband cried, but I didn't. I didn't cry again for seven years—after Jimmy died. I couldn't allow myself to cry, because if I did, it would all open up and I'd never stop and I'd break down and they'd have to 'take me away.' So I fought it. If I felt like crying, I'd go and talk to Jimmy, because I couldn't cry in front of him."

Once in a while, the reaction to the diagnosis may be almost one of recognition. A mother may have carried a kind of premonition that something was going to happen to this child, and the brooding mysterious weight of that lifts now that it's here, and she knows what she's facing.

Judy "always knew" that something would happen to healthy, cheery, sensible Christopher.

"When they were out playing and I heard a child scream, I'd say to myself, 'There you are, I told you. He's been hit by a car.' When he was diagnosed with leukemia at eight, I stopped being afraid."

As soon as Lily's teenage son was mildly ill, long before the blood tests, she "just knew" that he had cancer and that he would die. Everyone else was totally unprepared. They could not understand how Lily could accept it so calmly, as if she had known about it for a long time. She felt that she had.

Mary had a recurrent threatening dream from which she awoke in fear and tears: She fell with her son out of a high dormer window into a river, which swept the boy out of her arms. Years later, when she found herself in a bedroom under the roof at the house where she was staying while Joe was in treatment for Hodgkin's, she recognized the small-paned window and the stream that ran peaceably below the garden. Now that she understood what it meant, the dread of the dream went away.

After diagnosis, the urgent goal is to get the child into remission as soon as possible. Some can go home during the induction program, with frequent visits to the clinic. Others who live too far away or who are very sick, with swarming white cells crowding out the platelets and red cells, will be admitted to the hospital ward right away.

This completes the dizzying process of turning the family's life inside out in an alarmingly short space of time.

Yet when they look back to that so-recent time when everything was all right, it seems a lifetime ago. They can hardly remember what it was like not to know that something terrible had happened to their child, in that time of innocence, before it all began.

A ten-year-old is off-color, occasionally has a fever, is vaguely irritable, and has some bruises, as if she has been more clumsy than usual; she is tired all the time, flopping from one piece of furniture to the next.

Because this is not a family that rushes to doctors with every rise in temperature, the mother waits awhile before going to her pediatrician. An infection of some kind, he says. Let's try aspirin. Next time, he tries antibiotics. The mother hates putting pills of any kind into her children— if she could guess at the ferocious drugs that are ahead!— and when they don't bring the temperature down anyway, she goes back more anxiously to the doctor, who sends her to the local hospital for blood tests.

"No cause to worry, but it just could be mononucleosis, something like that."

Back at home, she and her daughter are reassuring each other, "At least if it's mono, we'll know what's wrong," when the phone rings. The doctor has never called her at home.

"Bring Susie back in. Call your husband at work and tell him to meet you here."

"Why?"

But she knows, in a way. Later, when the word *leukemia* has actually been spoken, to stay like a stain on the still air of the doctor's office, then she must allow herself completely to know, and nothing will ever be quite the same again.

Mass. General? *Now?* Hasty arrangements about the other children, the dogs, the spare tire.

"Don't call your mother yet."

"No. No one."

Some instinct tells them to keep this drawn secretly around them until they know what they are going to do with it.

Boston is three and a half hours away. They don't know the city. It is pouring rain, and they get lost. They don't know where to park. Will the Emergency Room know who Susie is, or what is wrong? What if they are too late to find this Dr. Truman they have been told to ask for?

As she steps out of the elevator onto the floor where Susie is to be admitted, the mother looks uncertainly at this unfamiliar world: strange faces, the clock on the wall, child-made decorations left over from Christmas, a bulletin board with children's pictures stuck all over it, a pile of charts askew on a littered desk, closed doors, doors half open, a bald child in a wheelchair being pushed slowly by a mother, who also pushes the intravenous pole on a wheeled stand.

Someone else's territory.

How odd, she thinks. Soon it will be mine. My feet will know the path between the elevator and Susie's door. I'll know where the extra pillows are kept, where to get coffee, which nurse is best to talk to, what happens when by that clock.

She and her husband are awake most of the night, talking, guessing, dozing in chairs, going to and from the cafeteria where the sandwiches will soon become so familiar,

24

walking down Cambridge Street to the river, past the gray stone jail that is like a barred fortress, hurrying back to the hospital in case Susie has woken.

In the morning there are more doctors and younger people who are fellows, residents, interns, nurse-practitioners—who is what? Soon the mother will be an expert on the whole hierarchy. Her husband has to go home, to his job, to the other children. By her third day and night here, this floor is completely her world.

Chapter T H R E E 🌿

When I was a nurse many years ago, the hospital world was like a secret society, and intrusive hovering mothers were considered a nuisance, even when their child was dying. Nowadays, most hospitals encourage parents to stay with their children, but it can be uncomfortable and exhausting to be there days and nights without a break. When you are there too long, because your child needs you all the time, or because you have nowhere else to stay, you take on a sort of hospital pallor, a gray, imprisoned look.

Depending on how sick your child is, you sleep in the room on a chair or cot bed, sometimes an empty ward bed if the nurse is not glued to the rules that say you can't, or you may doze fitfully on chairs or the floor of the day room. If you sleep in your child's room, the nurses come in and out all night, and if they don't, you worry. If you sleep outside the room, you wake up every hour to worry whether the nurse will call you if anything is wrong.

When David was admitted to the hospital ten years ago, he only had one chance in ten of surviving the first critical month. Deborah stayed with him day and night and became completely exhausted and not able to think straight.

"Go home with your husband," the nurses said to her each night. "The new baby needs you, and you need to rest."

The new baby was being securely cared for by a devoted neighbor with several daughters and was only upset when she was taken away from the attentive, motherly girls to go home with her father at night. And which is the worse way of exhausting yourself—to stay at the hospital all day and all night, or to lie awake at home, slobbering tears over the fists you bite to keep from waking the mercifully sleeping man beside you? Deborah stayed.

When friends wanted to come to the hospital, she wished they wouldn't. She didn't want them to see what had become of her beautiful boy. But when they did come anyway, she was glad. She thought she wanted to see her parents, but when they came, she thought they were only there because they believed that David was going to die. When she tried to talk about that, her mother said, "Don't say those things. I don't want to hear them."

Groping through a nightmare, Deborah did not know how to feel, how to think anymore.

When David was sent home with her for a few days, before the fateful month was over, his other grandmother had swabbed over his whole room and all his toys with Lysol.

"I wish your mother hadn't done that. Why did she have to do that?"

"You know he's lost his immunity to infection. She wanted to help."

"She wanted to criticize. She thinks my house is dirty."

"Debbie—that's not like you." Dave was a very equable young man. He didn't get angry. He got stunned and hurt.

"I'm not like me." Deborah had felt stunned since that evening in the windowless little room when the word *cancer* had come at her like a missile. "I don't know how to be."

Looking back on that time, she remembers very little of David's first weeks on the ward. She was in a fog most of the time, barely aware of visitors who came and went, passing other parents in the corridor with a blank look, hearing behind everything that was said to her the doctor's eight short weighted words:

"He may not make it through the month."

*　　*　　*

In the same hospital years later, Jerri was so lonely and tired one night that she crawled into bed with her sick daughter and was awakened at six by three young men coming in to examine the patient. If Jerri had been the patient, she would not have minded being caught in her underwear. As it was, she turned, speechless, to the wall and buried her head while the students prodded and peered and asked the questions that had been asked dozens of times by dozens of medical people of all ages and experience in the cause of healing this child, or other children in the future.

That night, Jerri's husband, Ed, came in from a hundred miles away after his shift as a policeman and took her to a seventy-dollar motel room. They stayed up the whole night talking and worrying and eating pizza and watching the fire trucks and police cars and ambulances that scream about Boston all night like crazed insects, especially in the streets around this large general hospital, which sees a hundred and fifty people in the Emergency Room every twenty-four hours.

The next night, Ed drove in after work and took Jerri home. As she walked into her house, the phone was ringing. Her daughter called three times, always in tears. They drove the hundred miles back to the hospital after midnight. Their daughter was asleep.

"Oh—" she said in the morning. "You came."

"Didn't you think I would?"

"Yes."

"I'll stay one more night then."

"And tomorrow night?"

Jerri stayed and overcame the exhaustion and loneliness by making the effort to break out of the shell of her miserable anxiety and find out what was going on with the other mothers.

Women who are fairly confident and outgoing can make friends on the ward, as they can in any other place, or pursue their natural bent for bolstering up someone else that is part of their mechanism for bolstering themselves.

Uncertain, diffident women who have had the pins knocked out from under them by what has happened feel isolated and foreign on the ward, although their citizen's passport, alas, is on the bed there, with the intravenous tubing leading into the skinny bruised arms.

To Clara, brought up by a pessimistic father who kept the blinds down and feared for his daughters and was suspicious of anyone who did not come from his own town in Italy, the other mothers were a threat. They were "different," noisier, quieter, warmer, colder than she could adjust to. There was no one she could talk to. Even when her amiable husband, who had rescued her gently from the narrow family cage, was with her in the hospital, she could not untie for him the hidden knot of panic and hopeless tears because they were propping each other up with "Maria's going to be *all right*."

To Louise, shy and self-doubting, her confidence sapped first by a divorce, then by her child's leukemia, which she imagined might be in some way her fault, it seemed as if all the other mothers were coping better than she was. Everyone was locked into their own concerns anyway, busy all the time with X-ray, cardiology, the eye clinic, the kidney specialist, hematology, medical checks before and after chemotherapy, lumbar punctures, spinals, IV bottles, visits from doctors, researchers, psychiatric social workers, answering questions, watching for the chance to ask their own, coaxing the child to eat, helping the child to throw up.

Penny, a free and easily joking woman, made a lot of friends in the hospital. It helped her to be talking to parents of children with other illnesses, to get away from cancer claustrophobia.

"And some of them were so much worse off. *Poor us,* I'd be thinking, but then these children with cystic fibrosis, wasting away, choking—that's a horrible thing. Cancer isn't really so horrible. We've been taught to think it is, and in those television plays where the child gets leukemia—easy bit of drama to throw in—it always dies. You spend time in the hospital here, and you see these mothers. . . . It's incredible what they do. What about the mothers of mentally retarded children? I couldn't cope with that."

Penny has two young daughters with sarcoma. One of them has lost a leg. The mothers of mentally retarded children probably think they couldn't cope with *that*.

But another mother told me, "Seeing someone worse off than yourself—that made me feel worse, not better. The first night I was on the ward, two babies died, just like that, plink, plink. I saw them taken away. The grandfather of one of them started to shout at the doctor. They gave him a shot of tranquilizer and took him away, still shouting.

"The next day, they said I should go to the parents' group meeting. I hated it. 'Get in touch with your feelings,' someone said. Feelings! There was a woman there whose child was bleeding to death upstairs. I couldn't take it. Later, I got so tough, I got so I could take just about anything I saw on the ward. After Billy almost died from Methotrexate poisoning, I went back to the group. It was helpful to me then. We talked about children losing their hair. That's the sort of thing people outside can't understand. Your child may die, and you're upset because he's going bald."

Every mother wants to stay with her child as much as she can, and no one should ever feel that the hospital resents them cluttering up the wards. At Mass. General, the ancient children's wards are cluttered and crowded anyway, so three or four parents in a three-bed room, with their cushions and knitting and books and radios and friends, don't make much difference.

The doctors and especially the nurses find it a tremendous help to have the family there. Mothers do practical things like make beds, bring milk shakes, wash and feed small children, and take them for wheelchair rides or walks with the ever-present IV pole on wheels. Many of the children have been admitted to the ward for an intensive course of very strong drugs that make them vomit, and they would get too dehydrated without the continuous intravenous drip.

On their first day, the parents of a new young patient were wringing their hands because they felt so lost and helpless. "What can we *do*?"

Kathy, one of the nurses, told them, "Sit with Kim while she vomits and hold the bowl and clean her up."

When Kim fell asleep at last and the parents tottered out of her room to take a break, Kathy said, "You passed the test. That was what she needed."

Kathy and the other nurses know that mostly what the children need is to have their mother or father there. Just to be there to share it. To tolerate the sadness of it calmly, so that the children won't have the extra anxiety of seeing what their illness has done to their parents.

David Harmon, a young doctor who helps Dr. Truman with his teenage cancer patients, has found the parents inspiring. "When people are really stressed, they come through with this sort of—greatness. I've learned a lot from them about how to live my own life. If I have children, I hope I'll have a better chance of doing it right."

He sees that even the parents who don't do so well at first—falling apart, complaining, upsetting the child—will usually get better as the situation gets worse. "They have what it takes, but it seems to take a crisis to bring it out."

Kathy, who is one of the nurses on the adolescent floor where the patients are from eight to eighteen, finds that the only problem with parents is when they become too protective. If there is over-mothering, if the son or daughter is never left alone, they don't get a chance to make friends with others on the ward and to feel they belong to this bizarre new world.

31

Sometimes overprotective parents who don't know how it works here will annoy both the child and the doctor by answering the questions the doctor asks the child. "He loves football." "He feels the pain worse at night." They soon drop that when they realize that, although Dr. Truman and Dr. Harmon will pay a lot of attention to them alone, when the child is present, that's who they want to talk to.

Some parents don't want a very ill child to know how bad it is. They want to shield a dying child from the truth, and they insist that the staff should not tell them.

But the child usually knows. So you have the sad situation where the parents can't talk honestly to the child, and the child can't talk to the parents because he thinks he's got to protect them.

"Do they *know*?" Donald asked Kathy, who had just been told by his mother outside the room, "I don't think he knows."

Kathy has a lovely candid face with soft eyes, wise and kind. She has learned, over her years in this kind of nursing, how to bring parents and children together and let them both know. "It's all right to talk about it. Tell each other. Cry. Share it."

These older children and teenagers can't always talk about what is troubling them, and the nurses have to take their chance when they can. At night sometimes their light keeps going on for juice, an extra blanket; "What time is it?" means "I'm lonely and I want to talk."

So Kathy will bring what they want and then stay to ask, "I wonder if there's something else?" If there is, she makes the time to stay with them. She will take in her paperwork and do it in the room, or call the supervisor for extra help, or ask another nurse, "Please watch my IVs, because something important is going on in Kim's room and I've got to stay with her."

The younger children obviously want at least one parent there as much as possible. This can be difficult enough

32

when there are two parents, but it is much worse when there is only one, and that one has a job, or other children at home, or lives far away.

Working mothers will often have to take leave from work, or even give up the job and try to manage on the Social Security payments to the sick child and some family help. After the child is discharged from the ward, they may have to stay away from work for months because of the frequent visits to the clinic.

Mothers who are recently divorced may not have got their life back together yet. Louise, who was dismayed and lost when she first became a hospital mother, thought that even a lousy husband might be better than no husband under these appalling circumstances.

"I can't go through this on my own." She called her ex-husband in Atlanta.

"He's doing all right, isn't he?"

"Yes, but . . . can you come to Boston?"

"I'll try," he said, but never did. "Give Ricky my love and tell him to be a good brave boy, and you let me know if it gets any worse, you hear?"

Divorced fathers don't often take much interest in a child with leukemia. Some will come back and help the child, but some will write it off as part of the marriage that is finished and won't want to get involved.

There are single fathers as well as single mothers on the wards and going in and out of Dr. Truman's clinic. Joe, who was divorced before blond, burly J.B. became sick at fifteen, has actually found it an advantage to be on his own. He has the kind of research job at a university where he can make his own hours and was able to stay with J.B. in the hospital "where each day is about a week long." He has liked the fact that when there were decisions to make he had only himself and J.B. to consult.

"After coming out of my second marriage, there was a wonderful calmness about being able to make instant decisions without all the talking back and forth and speculating and arguing and compromising. In severe trouble,

33

like J.B. and I have had, it seems so clear what has to be done. I've seen couples here, confused and terrified. Well— I was terrified, but I wasn't confused."

The father of Chris, another hefty blond fifteen-year-old, whose blondness is temporarily a wig, also knew what he had to do. After his marriage broke up, his children were in foster care because he was a crew member on a research ship and away at sea most of the time.

When Chris was diagnosed with leukemia, he changed his life and left the sea and got all three children back with him and got a job on land that allows him time off when he brings Chris to the clinic, which was every day for a month at first, and again the next year when Chris relapsed.

He and Chris seem to be very close.

Many of the teenagers come by themselves into the hospital for therapy, either because their parents are working, or because they want to do it that way.

Sometimes they want to do it, but they don't want to. David Harmon, who is their doctor, finds a lot of them rebellious, for several good reasons:

They are normal adolescents.

It's hard enough to make the perilous up-and-down journey through the teens without having to cope with cancer at the same time.

Chemotherapy and radiation make you feel sick. They don't make you feel better. "How do I know this awful stuff is helping?"

When they miss appointments, Dr. Harmon has to get after them. It's no good getting after the parents, because they probably can't control their teenager anyway. It's hard for the doctor to try to be an authority figure, since he's not that much older than his patients, who call him, not "Dr. Harmon," but "Hey, Dave!"

For Dr. Truman's patients who live within reasonable distance of Boston, the time on the ward and the endless clinic visits are difficult and exhausting, but workable. For those who come from farther away, it can be a tremendous burden that can sap their strength and their resources.

Some have come from other countries. I met mothers and children in the clinic from Bangladesh, South America, Spain, Israel. Some are from distant parts of New England, which means staying overnight for each visit, often for several nights, if there is intensive therapy going on.

These are people who live in a place where they can't get the specific treatment for the child's cancer, or who could use other hospitals, but choose to remain with their doctor and friends at the clinic, where they feel at home and secure.

"We could get the chemo and the radiation nearer home," one of them told me. "Dr. Truman offered to refer us, but I've got confidence in him. I didn't trust him at first. How could I trust *anybody* when my child might die and my world had just collapsed? It's different now. There's no one like him."

"I like it here. I love these people." Sally had to leave her husband and the other children in Spain to be here with Katie. "If John Truman is one of the best there is, we'll stick with that."

Peggy, who is divorced, left a baby and a three-year-old with her mother and father.

"Thank God they're young enough to adapt. I worry about my folks. They're too old to cope with this really. But they say what they couldn't cope with would be Buzz being so sick and them not able to do anything to help."

Marge, who was widowed only a year before her ten-year-old got sick, slept wherever she could on the ward for two weeks. Then she took a cheap and nasty room on the other side of the river for the daily clinic visits. When the money ran out, she stayed with a couple she had met at the hospital who let her and Amy sleep on the couch in the living room of their tiny apartment, in a heat wave.

"It was hell. For them too, I'm sure. They were marvelous."

A group of people who have been through this ordeal of being hospital parents themselves have planned and worked for several years to get a house going where families can stay while their child is in treatment at Mass. General.

The house is a five-minute walk from the hospital, a tall terraced house on Commonwealth Avenue in the Back Bay section, where the magnolias explode like bursts of white foam in the spring and joggers and lovers and old ladies with bad feet and people reading while they eat a sandwich lunch populate the green center strip.

The house is called Rest Inn Retreat. The idea for such a retreat originated when McDonald's, the fast-food chain, had the inspiration to start another kind of chain—family homes near the big children's hospitals all over the United States.

Like the Ronald McDonald houses, Rest Inn Retreat is comfortable and very cheap. There are about thirty beds, a lot of bathrooms, places to sit and talk or be quiet, noisy rooms for tots and teenagers, and, just as at home, the large kitchen is the focal point of the house.

The companionship is of that incomparable same-boat variety. The families understand and help each other. The house manager gives them jobs to do to make it seem like a home, not a hotel, and here they find the kind of comfortable, reassuring friendship that is hard to find in the tense, preoccupied world of the hospital. The women buy their own food and cook meals either separately or together. Anyone who is broke is invited unobtrusively to share.

Because Rest Inn Retreat was not yet open at the time I was talking to families, I went to the Boston Ronald

McDonald House near Children's Hospital to see how it works, and how much difference it makes to people pitched suddenly into crisis.

It is the proceeds not from the vast national corporation but from milk shakes and hamburgers in locally franchised restaurants that have bought and maintained the Victorian brick-and-plaster house in Brookline, stuck cozily about with gables and porches. There is a long wheelchair ramp where the front steps used to be when this was the stylish villa of a moneyed merchant in a prosperous part of the city.

The style is different now. The staircase is still broad and graceful, the paint is fresh, the carpets thick. Little skinny children who have lost their hair to the drugs that are keeping them alive play on the carpets. Pale teenagers with skin like fragile porcelain make music in the basement. The tired mothers putter about the bright kitchen and dining room, sit in deep chairs and tell each other things they would not say to anyone else ("Sometimes I don't want to do all this anymore"), or let another woman take their baby while they drag a body that has driven hundreds of miles and held the shrieking child through intravenous assaults and lumbar punctures up the graceful stairs to fall on a bed for the forgotten luxury of a daytime sleep.

Beth, who showed me around the house, told me what being there had done for her.

Shy Beth from northern Vermont, very young, using her big round glasses to hide behind as much as to see through, had hardly spoken to any of the other parents when she first went to Children's Hospital with Millie. This first child, not yet three, was to be operated on for a brain tumor.

At first her husband had refused to believe the bad news. After the CAT scan and the other tests at the local hospital, they both had to believe it, but Peter would never talk about it. Millie was getting worse. As soon as she got out of bed, she would vomit, sob hysterically, vomit again, then throw herself on the floor.

Beth thought she would go crazy. She couldn't bear what was happening. She would look at her daughter and see this thing that had invaded her head and she would want to scream and reach in to claw at it with her hands and wrench it out. When Peter came home she cried with relief at not being alone, but Peter would say, as he always did, "Don't cry."

He hated her to cry, and that made her cry harder, and he would ask, "Why do you have to cry? Why? Why?" and when she tried to tell him, "Millie might die," he would turn away. They were both in agony and both unable to help each other. She needed to weep and worry and talk. He needed to be left alone to shut it out, as if ignoring it by silence would make it go away.

When the time came for the operation, he could not leave his job, so Beth went alone with Millie on the plane from Vermont to Boston.

That night she stayed in the tiny room where the little girl slept in a crib as serenely as she did at home. The nurse had put up a cot bed for Beth. She sat up on it, not wanting to sleep, listening to the hospital night sounds, nurses' voices, bells, the whine of the elevator. *Is this me? Little country girl from upstate Vermont, how did it happen that so soon I'm part of this?* She heard the woman in the next room crying. *Should I go in? I don't know whether people do that.* The crying stopped. The woman's door opened and closed. *If she comes in here, I won't know what to say.*

Later, when she could not bear the cell any longer, she went outside, at least to see nurses moving and awake, even if she was afraid to talk to them. She saw the woman walking with a limp in the corridor, pale with long straight black hair, crying. The woman looked at her from her solitude, and Beth looked away. She could not talk to her. *I won't know what to say.*

A week after the operation, the doctor arranged for Beth

and Millie to move down the road to Ronald McDonald House. That evening Peter called, as he had called the hospital every night, hesitant, unsatisfying calls, important things not said and money wasted, like long-distance calls where people shout at each other across a continent questions about the weather.

When Beth went back to the comfortable room full of people, they looked up and smiled and one of them asked, "Everything all right?"

"Fine." Beth blushed. Then she saw that it was all right to say, "No, it's not. Peter gashed his finger at work. I wanted to talk about Millie's blood tests and the new drug and he only said, 'Oh sure,' like he does, dammit, as if he knew already. But he didn't know. That was why I was telling him."

Peter's habitual "Oh sure" response to her news had always offended her. She had never been able to tell anybody that. It was wonderful to unload it on this uncritical group, who seemed to understand and accept her. When she sat down, the woman in the next chair leaned over to give her a hug.

Beth and Millie stayed at the house for weeks, during radiation for the part of the brain tumor that could not have been surgically removed without killing or paralyzing the child.

Many other families came and went, and some of them came back again, but Beth had been there longer than anyone. In her granny spectacles, with her pale hair pulled up on her head in a lightweight cushion, shedding strands, she was the old lady of the house, welcoming new families, showing them where things were, helping to make them feel at home in what was now her home. She surprised herself, talking to strangers in a way she never had before, and discovered that other people could be shy and tongue-tied too. Now she was the one who asked "Everything all right?" when a mother came back rather uncertainly from a phone call.

Millie's radiation was the first morning appointment, so

they were back at the house by nine, helping the manager, whose child had also traveled through cancer, answering the phone, taking messages about rooms booked, canceled, the sudden change of plans that means you can't run Ronald House like a hotel, a doctor from the hospital asking: "Could you fit in two deaf parents, a teenager, and a newborn baby from Lebanon?"

Once when Beth was vacuuming the stairs, the front door opened and a woman who was from Nova Scotia came in, a fisherman's wife, dumpy, in a long skirt and old boots, her strong hair tugged back from a weathered face. Her son had Hodgkin's disease. He looked swollen and very ill. The woman was terrified. She would not share anybody's supper and could not say anything. Later that night when somebody was playing the piano, she came down in her boots, with a raincoat over her nightdress. When the music stopped, she was silent for half an hour, and then she suddenly began to talk, as if she had just discovered language.

When Beth and Millie came back from radiation, the woman from Nova Scotia was being given breakfast by someone with some eggs to spare.

"They said to be at the hospital by ten. How will we get there? Tony can't walk in the rain."

"You can call a cab. The numbers are up by the phone."

"Oh?" She looked blank.

Beth said, "I'll get one for you."

The woman had never been in a taxi. Beth left Millie with someone and went with her in the taxi and up to the ward, where she was greeted as an old friend by nurses she had not thought would remember her. The next day she took the woman from Nova Scotia all over the complicated hospital and through the tunnel to the cancer clinic, showing her all the places she would need to know.

"But her boy died, you know. Pneumonia. I took her to the airport. Her husband was at sea. He couldn't get

40

away to fetch her. Peter is coming to get us next week, if the scan shows the tumor is dissolved, or at least no bigger. It will be so odd being married again. I dunno. I've hardly seen Peter for months. It's weird though, how little you know a person. Last time he was here, when Millie was real sick again and we didn't know if she'd make it, he still wouldn't talk about it. I only found out after, that he'd told the doctor about how he was so worried about her and me both.

"So I go, 'Why didn't you talk to me?'

"And he goes, 'I didn't want to upset you.' Oh, dammit, he thought I . . . and I thought he didn't . . . I mean, why can't we ever really *talk*? We never talk about anything except the cost of things and what his mother thinks and what it says on the radio. Perhaps we will now. Yeah, I guess. Maybe I can teach him, now that I've learned myself. Maybe not."

Ronald House is only for families of children with cancer at Children's Hospital. Rest Inn Retreat is for the families of any child patient at Mass. General, and in its practical caring, it is a landmark in the long history of this hospital. There will be many Beths and Millies who will find sanctuary there, and lost people like the woman from Nova Scotia, and families of all sorts in all sorts of situations whose distress will be eased.

"We needed this house desperately," Dr. Truman says. "For so many families up to now, it's been fragmenting, uncivilizing, like tenting in the Adirondacks without a tent. It's impossible to take care of parents in the hospital in the way we should. And they're so important. They're my allies. They matter to the child's treatment, at every stage of everything we do."

This dedicated group of parents have worked and fought and schemed for five years, through discouragement and disappointment, to get their Rest Inn Retreat house going. It wasn't easy. No one took them seriously at first. They had no money, no influence, no experience, not much but a rather desperate determination to make things better for future families than it had been for them.

Some of them got involved in the struggle for the house because of gratitude for a child who lived, some because of the memory of one who did not. Barbara and Sheila were the mothers who started it, after Brian and Mark died, within a few months of each other, from Hodgkin's disease and bone cancer.

How can one make anything at all positive out of disaster? It isn't possible at first. You can't look beyond your own sorrow. It takes time to be able to turn back to the sick world you have left and try to help someone who is still trapped in it. It takes awhile before you can look at what has been gained along with the loss: new friendships, a closer love, clearer understanding.

Whether your child has survived the ordeal or not, it can take a long time to realize that you seem somehow to have changed for the better.

But people change anyway, you reason. I'm supposed to develop. I didn't have to go through hell. . . .

Don't tell me suffering is good for you. It's not. It is evil, cruel, destructive, narrowing. It brings self-pity and bitterness. It crowds out joy. Where is my silly happiness? I've got so *old*.

All right then, I have changed. Good things can come out of bad. But what about my child's suffering? What good has come out of that?

If only my child's suffering could mean that no other child need suffer!

Research, new knowledge about how the drugs work, why one body can't destroy the first wild cells and others can: each child with cancer may add a tiny piece to the sum total of an eventual cure. I know all that. It's not the point. It doesn't approach the essential meaning. We clutch, grasp—it's out of reach.

"If only my son's death could mean that no other child need die!"

That's what it would take, I heard the father cry. Nothing else will do.

I die that you may live. What else could Christ offer? It was the only thing that was enough. The only acceptable promise.

Chapter F O U R 🌿

Whether your child is in the hospital or being treated in the clinic, everyone is working toward the goal of a stabilized white cell count, which means that the chemotherapy has knocked out the cancer cells in the blood and the child is in remission.

That usually takes about four weeks, depending on the severity and type of the leukemia, and then the maintenance program starts to keep the abnormal cells from reappearing.

Nowadays, not everyone is admitted to the ward after diagnosis. Children who need continuous intravenous infusion or especially powerful drugs must stay on the ward. If the white cell count is very high, with severe symptoms, so many of the invading cells must be killed so quickly that getting rid of them through the excreting mechanism of the kidneys can be almost more than a small body can handle. The child may have to be in the Pediatric Intensive Care Unit, known as PICU, pronounced "Pick-you."

Children who are not so sick can start as carefully monitored outpatients if they live near enough to come to the clinic frequently, or can stay with friends or family in Boston or at Rest Inn Retreat.

Twelve years ago, when Deborah first brought David to Mass. General, everyone with leukemia was admitted to the ward. Less was known then about how the drugs worked, and remission was harder to induce, which was why David's chances were worse then than they would be now for a two-year-old with acute lymphocytic leukemia, known as ALL.

He did make it through that first critical month, and after he was in remission his mother was able to take him home from the hospital, at first for weekends, then all the time.

You long for the day when you and your child can be gone from the ward, but when they tell you, "Take him home," it suddenly seems too soon. He isn't ready. You are not ready to carry the whole responsibility.

And where is everybody? When she got home, Deborah had lost not only the nurses and young residents and interns, and seeing Dr. Truman two or three times a day, but most of her friends and neighbors as well, it seemed.

Since David's immune system had been weakened by the drugs, those neighbors with children were staying away for fear of infection, but others stayed clear because they did not know what to say. Deborah saw them cross the street to avoid her, or dodge into another aisle at the supermarket.

In the post office, she bumped into a friend who burst into tears, gasped, "I don't know what to say to you!" and ran away. A neighbor informed her that lightning never strikes twice in the same place. "Your son got it, so mine won't."

"It" was sometimes referred to as leukemia. Never as cancer. "Leukemia is only a blood disease . . . isn't it?"

So Deborah, like thousands of mothers before her and since, found herself with the extra burden of consoling people who should have been consoling her, and who might have liked to, if they had known how.

They never asked her how she was. At the occasional parties to which she and Dave made themselves go so as not to be consumed by the illness, it was, "How's everything?" and sometimes, "How's David doing?" Never—perhaps because her husband still had his hopeful smile and Deborah was as beautiful as ever, with her hair always clean and curling on her shoulders—"How are *you* doing?"

There were times when Deborah wanted to stop being brave and beautiful and cry in an ugly public way and tell everybody how she really felt. Mostly she cried alone in the car, a safe place for mothers to scream and pull their mouths about because they are afraid and worn out.

One close and true friend, and maybe that's enough— some people don't even have one—did not worry about what to say. She was the neighbor with the motherly daughters who was giving the practical help of looking after the baby every time Deborah had to take David to the hospital.

In those days, Dr. Truman did not have his own clinic. Although he was specializing in childhood cancer and blood diseases, he was still in a tiny office high up in an old part of the hospital where he had started general practice with children.

Deborah was frightened the first time she took David there as an outpatient. Going up in an old elevator, its walls scarred by years of stretchers and food wagons, she thought wildly, "What am I doing here? David can't really have cancer. He never did. It's a mistake." In the tiny, crowded waiting room, there was only one chair left for her to sit in with David on her knee. The other women knew each other. They talked like club members.

"Dr. Truman's had her in again and again with strep throat, staph infection, spiking a temp. . . ."

Oh yes, the other mothers nodded. They knew.

"He acted so horrible last time, but Dr. Truman made a joke of it, you know how he is."

Oh yes, they knew.

"Jeff was exposed to Father O'Riley's shingles when he made his first communion. If he gets chicken pox, Dr. Truman says . . ."

Deborah got up and put David on the chair, where he slid to the floor to aim his ingratiating smile at a Chinese child. He was not afraid. Deborah was. She did not belong here. Dr. Truman, who had saved David's life in the hospital, was not her property anymore. He had all these other patients who knew him better than she did, and who were engulfing his time and energy. He would not care about her and David.

She had to get out. She took David's hand. He was standing with his new friend by the Chinese mother's knee, looking at pictures, but she pulled him out of the room. In the corridor, she couldn't find the way out.

A nurse said, "David? Come on in."

Dr. Truman sat behind a desk in an ordinary suit instead of his white ward coat, and Deborah wanted to walk right past him and on out the eleventh-floor window.

Sitting in front of the desk, trying to listen to the program he was explaining—injections, pills, cranial radiation, David would lose more of his hair—she pretended to herself that the doctor was cold and detached, to explain her fear and resentment. He was only nine years older than she, but she saw him as a stern patriarch, condemning her to months and months of poisonous chemicals and dangerous rays and endless clinic visits.

I'll never go through with it. Those other mothers are different.

"Clinic visits?"

"We've outgrown this place," the doctor was saying. "We're starting a specific clinic for all of you."

A clinic—what's that? In her confusion, Deborah saw it as a place for down-and-outs and degenerates, shuffling hopelessly through.

As it turned out, David was the first patient in the new clinic. He was famous for that, as well as for being a beautiful, blond, happy child, beloved of everybody, loving everybody, and making the hospital his playground.

Some of the ward nurses took turns working in the clinic so that the children and their families would find old friends. John Truman did not seem like Deborah's father anymore.

47

The other mothers turned out to be the same as her, with the same kind of fears and need for friendship. One mother from Europe told her that she had suffered the same reaction to the word *clinic*. "All I could think of was a concentration camp."

Her husband Dave came to the clinic too, when he could leave work, and he and Deborah made friends with other parents in this willy-nilly association of survivors in a lifeboat. Over the months and years of therapy, the clinic became familiar and quite homey.

When the patients outgrew this place too, and the clinic was moved to brand-new rooms in a sunny corner of a new building, the old pioneers like Deborah, who used to complain that the original clinic was cramped and old-fashioned, felt nostalgia for it, as people do when you improve their surroundings.

The families who started their careers as outpatients in this new clinic have in their turn established hominess here and would no doubt resent the next move if this place were ever outgrown.

At present, that's unlikely. They are managing to treat a great number of children and teenagers, and they don't want to expand and lose the very close personal attachments that get formed here.

The basic maintenance therapy has not changed very much since Deborah was a clinic mother, except for differences in the combinations of drugs given.

The program of drugs and hospital visits for blood tests and lumbar punctures and bone marrow biopsies is different for each child, according to need. The drugs are given orally at home, or in the clinic by IV or injection, or directly into the spinal fluid to reach the brain. For patients outside Boston, simple injections can be given by a local doctor. Cranial radiation is not routinely given at Mass. General now, unless there is a relapse or evidence of invasion of the central nervous system.

New techniques for extracting platelets from donated

whole blood have dramatically reduced the risk of hemorrhages. The platelets, the blood's clotting factor, can be given to the patient, which makes it possible to use more aggressive drugs that may rob the red cells of their own platelets.

The names of the drugs that become so depressingly familiar sound bizarre at first—Vincristine, Danorubicin, Adriamycin, Asparaginase—like characters in a crudely imagined fairy tale.

"I'd rather they were called Strongheart or Galahad," a nineteen-year-old mother ruminated wistfully.

Let's look at a typical day for Dr. Truman and his staff, if you can call any of them typical. They all vary, depending on who comes in and what is happening on the wards. There are packed days and more relaxed days, crises and sorrows and long hard satisfying days, and days of rejoicing.

For every patient or parent coming in past Cindy's office window in the corridor to the crowded central space, wallpapered with pictures of children, and through to the big treatment room, all windows and light, the welcome is the same. You are the one person they wanted to see that day.

"Phenomenal," J.B.'s father said. "Some of the doctors and nurses when my wife was ill—they were so brisk and condescending. These people act as if you were doing them the greatest favor."

"When you're with John Truman," Katie's father said, "he behaves as if you were the only person he had to see that day."

At the early morning meeting are Dr. Truman, Sue, Monica, David Harmon (the doctor who works with some of the older children), a nurse from the ward who is following up some of the patients she cared for on Burnham 4, Steve, a medical student, and Bill Ferguson, the current fellow, a young doctor doing special training in pediatric hematology.

We crowd into a corner of the treatment room. John Truman goes to fetch a couple of extra chairs. The ward nurse sits on the high bed, dangling legs that look good even in thick white nylon. Dr. Truman, who tends to look as if he had just come from a soapy bath, a barber, and a dry cleaner, wears a spruce gray suit and white shirt and polished shoes, which is the way you always see him. Last year he joined in a sponsored walk for leukemia research organized by two of the parents who had lost a child and was given a special prize for being the only man who walked five miles wearing a tie.

Sue and Monica don't wear white coats or uniforms. They wear ordinary clothes, attractive, with bright colors. Bill wears crumpled chino pants, which descend below his waist and need to be hitched up with hands in pockets. Steve wears a crumpled white hospital coat with someone else's name on the pocket. He is a student from Boston University Medical School doing some elective time here. Apart from wanting to work with Dr. Truman, this clinic suits him better than a larger, more organized cancer center.

"Well, sorry, I mean—this is organized. But it's more relaxed and personal. And the food is better."

There are always cakes and cookies and nuts and candy by the coffee machine, mostly brought in by parents. Between the young patients and the families and the staff, everything is always gone by the end of the day.

John Truman describes the patients of this day for the benefit of those of us who don't know them as Sue and Monica do (I'll leave out their last names here).

"We're going to see Michael. He's a young man who, five years ago, was found to have cancer of the sympathetic nerves. That usually shows in the abdomen. His was a huge mass in the neck, which was removed in a gigantic piece of surgery. Then he came to us for chemotherapy. The surgeon did a brilliant job, but I'd have preferred Michael to be treated with chemo first, then surgery when the mass was smaller."

"Why wasn't he?"

"Because, Steve, he was referred to a surgeon first. So in the contest between medical and surgical treatment, the surgeon won."

This is obviously a familiar and serious contest, but Dr. Truman is still smiling gently, because that is the way his face is made.

" 'If it's cancer, take it out' was the surgeon's philosophy. Mine is, there are other ways. You do what's least mutilating. In the U.K.," he adds wistfully, "parents aren't usually referred directly to surgeons. The physicians can tell the surgeons what they want done.

"Chris is coming in for a spinal. His father's a great fellow, left the sea, got custody of his children, has seen Chris through this whole thing, including a relapse after three years of remission."

Cindy looks in. "Charlotte is here with the baby. Does she need a chest X-ray?"

"Yes, she does."

Monica adds, "Tell her to come back up here afterward so we can see the baby."

Dr. Truman reminisces with Monica about Charlotte's romance and marriage in the teeth of some family opposition because she was still sick, and what her mother said when she got pregnant, and so on. He and Monica and Sue know and remember a lot about all the patients and their families. "You're not just a patient here," many of the mothers have told me, "only interesting because of the illness. They care about what your life is like outside the hospital."

"Young Jason is coming in for a spinal. Bill, if you would do that . . . no problems. He's doing well."

"His mother is going to have another baby. That'll be four under six years old."

"Amazing young woman. A new patient—Donald. He's been referred to us for confirmation of infectious mononucleosis. The odds are that his low platelet count is related to viral infection, but it just could be leukemia, so we have to do a bone marrow."

Sue and Monica are called out to speak to parents on the phone and in the clinic. People are arriving, being greeted. "How lovely to see you!" Someone laughs. Someone is throwing a tantrum.

"J.B. is coming in for a spinal. Poor fellow, he hates it. But he always comes. At eighteen, he's so tough and musclebound, it's like trying to get into the shell of a turtle. Elizabeth, the fellow before you, Bill, was the only one who could do it right for him. So I wrote and asked her, 'What's the secret of getting into J.B.?' I tried what she said, and by God, it did work better."

"She do it differently?" David Harmon asks.

"A bit. She's also better looking."

David's beeper goes off and he goes out to the phone. He comes back. "I'm going to Burnham 6."

"Robert?"

"It doesn't look as if he's going to make it through the day. All his family are there."

"How long since we first saw him?"

"Before my time. About thirteen years. It's amazing he's lasted as long as this."

A small, sad silence.

Then they must go back to the living. "Harriet. Six weeks after remission, and there's no sign of the enemy. Polly is coming in. Also doing well. She lives in Bangladesh and would have relapsed and probably died if her brother hadn't brought her over here. Remember how she looked? A poor, shivering, frightened, sickly little girl, all eyes, huddled in a corner of the bed. She's now outgoing, cheerful, healthy. A joy to look at her."

Sue comes back. "Lauren's mother wants her to come in. Poor kid, she spends half her time in here."

Rosa will bring herself in. She lives in one of the rottener housing projects in Boston, in a totally chaotic and fragmented family with many children of various fathers.

"Poor Rosa has leukemia in the midst of all this chaos.

Yet she's just like a little rock. Takes her medications. Never misses an appointment. At thirteen, she's the only solid person in the family."

The pediatric hematology unit of another Boston hospital has had to close, and twenty or thirty of its patients are going to be fitted in here to the already busy program. One of the new families will come in today. So will Jill, a new patient who came to the Emergency Room on Friday and was kept on Burnham 4 over the weekend. She has chronic myelocytic leukemia, a type very rare in children and very deceptive.

"Jill doesn't look sick or feel sick. They only found her enlarged spleen and astronomical white cell count because her mother was worried enough about a bruise to take her to a doctor, thank God. But I'm afraid this chronic phase will, in six months to two years, suddenly erupt into the accelerated phase, which will be almost impossible for us to control. So from this gentle beginning . . ." He shakes his head. "She has a sister, so we'll try for a bone marrow transplant."

Three small patients with "Mediterranean anemia" will be in for their monthly blood transfusions. Mediterranean anemia is correctly called thalassemia, from *thalassos,* the sea. The disease is found in places like Greece, Italy, the Middle East, China, and across the equator, and it is thought to have developed long ago as a protection against malaria, much like sickle-cell anemia. It can be fatal if not treated with blood transfusions every three or four weeks for the rest of the child's life. It's a nonmalignancy that can be as bad as a malignancy, with no end in sight.

"And Joanne, who brought us the pound cake. She has ALL, off chemotherapy for a year. In the four years we've known her, she's never said a word to any of us. But her mother swears she chatters away at home. Okay then, to work. Bill, you check out Michael. I'll join you and then we'll talk to Donald's family. They hadn't suspected leukemia, but by now they probably do."

Cindy now has several people in the clinic, distributed

in the small rooms or waiting to come into the treatment room, which has four beds, a lot of toys, and a videotape player, which adds to the general racket when the room is full of patients and parents.

A square blond boy of about five comes confidently in ahead of his mother, his cheeks fat from prednisone, a deep solemn voice. Monica bends to kiss him. Dr. Truman sticks out a hand and says, "Put it there, old bean."

"Can I watch *Annie*?" Jason asks.

"Sure. Ask Sue to put it on for you."

The morning program gets underway. There are times when there are so many people in the clinic and waiting room that it doesn't seem possible they will get through everyone; but a lot of the crowd are parents or brothers or sisters or friends who come to support the child and are always welcome.

Bill and Sue do a spinal on Chris. Steve and Monica do a bone marrow biopsy from the iliac crest of Donald's pelvis. A tiny Italian child who lost his sight through too much oxygen as a premature baby is on the corner bed, where Monica sets up his blood transfusion. Around the bed are his parents and two other people who croon to him and tell him what's going on—"*Mama e qui!*" "*Questa Monica!*"—and chatter in Italian, while *Annie* chatters away on the television screen, watched solemnly by Jason, who knows the movie by heart and tells his mother what's going to happen. She sits in a smock with some sewing by the bed on which he sits, brawny and barechested like a miniature potentate, while the Italians shout and laugh and sing to the little boy in the corner.

Jeff, who is about twelve, climbs onto a vacant bed in the other corner. Sue comes in to find out whether he's taking all his pills and whether they're still making him vomit.

"How are *you* doing?" she asks his mother, who looks tired and untidy.

"Hanging in there." The mother laughs. "Some days my

54

husband says Jeff's doing better than me. *I* say"—she nods at her son who is chewing gum and listening nonchalantly—"it's a good thing it's him who has the cancer. If it was me, I'd shoot myself." The boy looks at her tolerantly and shrugs. "I have a hard enough time being his mother. It took me ages even to learn to drive in Boston."

"So it did me," says Jason's small pretty mother, whose mouth is serene but whose eyes are sad beyond their years. "We live in New Hampshire. I'd never even been to Boston. If I'd been told years ago I'd learn to drive a gearshift car a hundred miles each way and through all the city traffic, I'd have said, 'Forget it.' Now I can't believe all the things I can do."

"I help you, Mum," Jason says in his deep, solemn voice.

Sue hugs him, and he wriggles away, to keep his eyes on the screen. He protests when she wheels in the table for his spinal and draws the curtain.

"You can keep listening to the song. This will only take a minute."

"Tomorrow, tomorrow . . ." Annie bawls from the screen. Jason, with his deep voice and manly ways, begins to cry like an outraged baby.

Steve has looked at Donald's bone marrow sample through the microscope. He gives his opinion, and then the doctors look at it. Cindy has been sitting out in the waiting room with Donald's parents, who are very nervous. They come in white-faced, to be told, "It's definitely not leukemia," and leave smiling, planning where they will go for lunch.

Charlotte comes up from X-ray to display the baby. A tall teenager with a scarf over her bald head, who has been in remission for six weeks, comes in to be told, "The enemy has been defeated in the first battle. Now we'll go after him all the way."

J.B. has been waiting with his father Joe in one of the small rooms, not talking, his big strong hands clenched, beginning to sweat with fear of the spinal. The jab of the lumbar puncture is very quick. Often the Novocain needle hurts more. But he hates the humiliating, vulnerable way he has to lie, curled up with his father hanging on to his neck and knees to bend his powerful body. What's going on behind his back? When is it going to zap him? He grits his teeth and a great groan is ground out from between them.

Joe is one of the few fathers who is able to stand up and watch a spinal or a bone marrow biopsy. The mothers stand, but the fathers usually sit so they can pretend to bend down to tie their shoe if they feel faint, and they won't have so far to fall if they pass out.

Having to see your child put through pain and trauma can be a worse agony than having to go through it yourself. You want to bear it for them, but you can't.

Monica is looking for Lauren to get some blood for tests. Lauren has gone to telephone Sue's boyfriend at work. He and Sue take Lauren on trips to places like the Aquarium and the Museum of Science, and she often calls him. She comes running back down the long corridor and through the open door of the clinic, pale red hair, pale skin, invisible lashes and eyebrows, and hurtles at Monica and hugs her.

"*Oh,* you are a lovely girl."

"I feel terrible." Lauren pulls down her face, needing sympathy. "My back aches, and I'm so sick of it all."

"I'm glad you came in."

"So am I."

Lauren and Monica go off to find a vacant room, arms around each other's waists.

Jill and her parents are here. They go into Dr. Truman's office with Sue and Bill. He was in the Emergency Room when they first came in, so he is at least a slightly familiar face in this alien new country into which they have suddenly been pitched.

They sit with Jill facing the doctor. Bill leans against the wall, his baggy trousers pulled down on one side by the beeper clipped to the pocket. Sue sits on the roof of a

56

dollhouse that has found its way into the doctor's office and stayed there.

Jill's parents Tony and Paula are suffering, but are amazingly calm and sensible: he, a good-looking young father with dark Italian eyes and a forehead anxiously creased; she, a tall, gentle mother with her head tilted wistfully on her long neck and her eyes fixed on the doctor, watching his face for the truth; Jill, a thin, pale, eager girl of eleven with delicate slim hands, a ready smile around big teeth she hasn't yet grown into, and beautiful dark eyes and winged eyebrows.

Jill is very social and caring. She has made friends with everyone on the ward. When Dr. Truman tells her that she can go home today, she says at once, "I can't go yet. Kim needs me. She only has one leg now, you know."

"I know, but I think Kim is going home too."

"Isn't it too soon after her operation?"

"I don't think so. She wants to go back to school."

"So do I."

"I hope you can go back soon, if you stick to your medication. You'll be on one pill a day for a while. That's all."

He is speaking to all of them, but he speaks and looks at Jill. He shows her a chart with a picture of her pill on it, green and pink. She listens carefully and asks intelligent questions. "Will it make me throw up? Can I eat what I want? Will I lose my hair?"

"I'm afraid you may later, when you have more chemo-therapy."

"That's all right," Jill says quickly, before she can think about it. "Will you buy me a wig?" she asks her mother.

"Of course, if you want it."

"I can take it off to wash. Be much easier." She flips her straight dark hair back and forth over her shoulder and strokes it. It won't be all right to lose it, but she is being as heroic as her parents.

Jill goes out with Sue to have a blood sample taken. She is wearing a T-shirt with a few notes of music on it and the name of the hit song "Beat It," which can be interpreted as heroic too.

"She looks so *well*." Paula's face relaxes into distress after Jill goes out. "But she's different. She's usually very quick and smart. She had everything worked out. Now she's sort of vague and lost. Her whole life has changed in four days. She's overwhelmed."

"A high white cell count can cause some memory loss."

"Then we're not imagining things?" Tony asks. "We don't want to get too protective, but if she stumbles or bumps her head now, we panic. How ill is she?"

"She's in the chronic stage now, but it can get nasty in the long run."

"How long is the long run?"

"We'll be able to predict as time goes on. Four months—six months, perhaps."

"Is that when she would have the bone marrow transplant?" Paula asks. Dr. Truman has talked to them about the substitution of healthy bone marrow for Jill's marrow that carries the cancer cells.

"If there's a donor. As soon as the disease starts to accelerate. No later. Maybe earlier, in this quiet phase. I'm going to consult some of the transplant centers about that."

"What if her younger sister can't be a donor?"

"We have two options. We can consult the tissue-typing bank in Iowa to try to find an unrelated donor, or we could harvest Jill's marrow in this stable chronic phase and freeze it until it's needed. Then after massive chemotherapy and total body irradiation to get rid of all the diseased marrow, the transplant will put her back to where she is now. But if there's a donor"—he smiles at both of them—"we'll try for a cure."

"A cure." Paula catches her breath and says intensely, "*I want that word*."

"There's a twenty-five percent chance her sister can be the donor. But let's not tell her why she's coming in for the tissue typing, so she won't feel she's failed if she's not a match."

"Everything hangs on it, doesn't it?" Paula says.

"Everything."

There is a short silence. Jill has left her bright living presence in this room, to fill everyone's thoughts. Then the parents get up and wander out. Bill sighs and pushes himself upright off the wall and rubs his hand over his face to loosen the tension. Dr. Truman gets up and stands for a moment in what one of the mothers calls "Dr. Truman's posture," long arms folded, holding them above the elbows; then he follows the parents out of the room.

Sue tells them they will find Jill on the ward with Kim. The doctor will go with them. "I have to see Kim and her family, Sue, and I'm going to check the CAT scans on Dennis and see him too."

The clinic is emptying out. The Italian family has left, leaving a new photograph of the little blind boy, holding his face up to the sun and laughing, pinned on the wall. Monica is going down to the cafeteria for lunch with Steve, to answer some questions for him. Sue puts on a white gown and rubber gloves and prepares an injection under the laminar air flow hood, which is a protection against potential risk from exposure to the strong chemicals.

The mother from Israel holds her daughter on her lap, milky skin, a fine little sensitive face. The mother shields her eyes. The child's hand is like a transparent shell. Sue ties rubber tubing around her arm, rubs the back of her hand, and deftly slips the tiny butterfly needle into a raised blue vein and fits the syringe into it, while the woman and the child commiserate with each other in Hebrew.

In Dennis's room, the eleven-year-old boy sits on a chair at the foot of the bed. His mother sits on his bed, patient, steady, an initiated hospital mother. Two or three un-identified friends stand about. The surgeon sits on the other bed wearing green operating clothes. Dr. Truman comes amiably as far as he can get into the narrow, crowded room.

Dennis has Hodgkin's disease. The CAT scan shows that

59

the large lymph nodes in his neck and chest are back to normal. Now he will have his spleen removed, which is standard in Hodgkin's, and an exploratory operation to see if there are diseased nodes below the diaphragm.

His mother asks serious commonsense questions about the laparotomy operation and the follow-up treatment. Dennis looks scared. He leans over to take a pillow from the bed and hug it on his lap over the places they are talking about.

The surgeon, who is genial, says it will be no worse than an appendix operation. A week in the hospital and back to school in ten days.

"And playing golf." He laughs. "Here's a bad joke for you. If you don't play golf before the surgery, it won't improve your game." Well, he's trying.

Dr. Truman adds that Dennis will need penicillin twice a day until his early twenties.

Dennis, scornfully: "Penicillin is *mold*." He is angry. He doesn't say anymore.

Outside in the corridor of Burnham 4, Jill's mother says good-bye to another mother she has spoken to over the weekend.

"Are you all right?" The other mother looks at her perceptively.

Paula nods. "Sorry I wasn't more friendly. I was afraid. I didn't know what to do. This thing had just hit us, and I didn't feel any of us belonged here."

Jill seems to belong. She is pushing her friend Kim in a wheelchair. Kim has one trouser leg tied in a knot above the knee where her leg has been amputated because of osteosarcoma. When Jill first came to the ward, her initial reaction to seeing Kim had been to tell her mother, "How funny. They tied her leg in a knot."

She pushes Kim into the four-bed room where Kim's mother is sitting on her bed, two older sisters are hanging about, and her father is trying out Kim's crutches. By another bed, a father sits reading to a dozing girl who is having an intravenous infusion.

Jill goes to the far bed to turn on the radio and play with a smaller girl and some dolls. A nurse comes in and hooks up an IV to the hand of the small girl, who goes on giggling with Jill and takes no notice. Sally, the teacher and occupational therapist who keeps the less ill patients busy almost all day long, comes in to bring Jill some pictures she made.

Dr. Truman moves, smiling, into the turmoil of the room and finds a chair. Kim's father sits beside his wife on the bed, both looking anxious, and the largest of the sisters takes the crutches and uses them as a prop while she stands and listens.

Kim leans forward in her chair, hair falling over her face, sucking a lollipop and listening to Dr. Truman.

"*So.* We must start chemotherapy to kill any wandering cells. Osteosarcoma needs six different drugs. Sometimes you'll get a shot in the clinic. Sometimes you'll have them here in the ward. About sixteen times during the next year, you'll come in for IVs for two or three nights. The whole course takes forty-three weeks, and the hospital will be your second home."

He shows Kim a chart and tells her slowly and carefully the names of the drugs and the dates they will start.

"Your hair will begin to fall out in about six weeks." Kim nods calmly. "People wear either a cap or a wig."

"A wig," Kim tells her father.

The doctor explains to all of them that consent is needed for the high dose of Methotrexate and talks about the side effects. "No one has all of them. Everybody has some. The kidneys could be affected, though that's rare. Also the heart, so you'll have regular EKGs. Vomiting always, I'm afraid."

The family listens. Kim's father is rather red in the face and looks as if he might cry. "Make an appointment with Cindy to come back in three days to start the Methotrexate, and I'll be here then for your questions."

The parents nod and thank him. They are quiet and stoic. (Their child lost her leg only a week ago.) Everyone says that Kim has been "marvelous." They are so proud of her.

Kim looks up at Dr. Truman and then looks down. She looks at her hands holding the lollipop stick and then looks at the knot in her green trousers.

Jill pushes her into the playroom to say good-bye to Sally and the people there. Then Paula and Tony take Jill away, looking back over her shoulder, and Kim's father pushes her toward the elevators.

From behind the central desks where nurses, doctors, residents, students, secretaries, and others mill about among papers and files and telephones, Kathy, Kim's primary nurse, comes out. She bends to kiss Kim, and Kim reaches up to hug her.

Three days before the operation, Kim had talked about it quite casually. "I have to have my leg cut off." Kathy told her to say good-bye to it, but it wasn't real until she came back from the operating room and didn't see her leg.

Yesterday she had cried and sobbed to Kathy, "I miss my leg, I want it back. I want to be normal again."

"You are normal. You are just the same as everybody else, only a bit nicer than some."

"I don't want to be special. I don't want any more presents and visits and treats and people telling me I'm marvelous and doing things for me. I want to do things for myself. I want to be able to be—*competent* again."

That was her word, at twelve years old. Competent.

Before Kim went back to school, Sue was asked to talk to about a hundred of her fellow students in the seventh and eighth grades.

She told them about the different types of cancer and how it was treated—chemotherapy, radiation, surgery. She told them about Kim's kind of bone cancer and why it had been necessary to amputate her leg.

For most of the hour, she answered questions.

Where was the leg cut off? How did they stop it bleeding? What does it look like? Where is the leg now? What do we say to Kim? Do we help her up if she falls or pretend not to see? Can she bend the artificial leg? Will it fall off? How is it stuck on? Did they sew hooks in her thigh or what? What causes cancer? Will I get it?

A girl sitting apart, a loner, asked, "Did Jill ever think about committing suicide?"

"I don't think so. Would you?"

The girl nodded, chin in hand.

In the clinic, Dr. Truman has gone for a late lunch with one of the doctors who is sending him two dozen patients from the other hospital. Two more thalassemia patients are in for their transfusions. They are both Greek, accompanied by squads of family and supporters. *Mary Poppins* is showing on the screen.

Betty comes in to say hello. She's a young pianist from Brazil who originally came to Boston for diagnosis and treatment of a facial sarcoma. She stayed here to go to music school, and Dr. Truman and Sue went to her first recital.

Lauren, who is waiting for her mother, is lying down in one of the small rooms. Cindy goes to chat with her and make jokes, and lets her grouse, which is what she seems to need to do today. She needs to say ugly things about the drug Vincristine, so they make up a terrible poem about it and laugh together.

When she leaves, Cindy gets back to her paperwork. A father comes in from an office in Government Center for a new prednisone prescription, and Cindy, who knows all the shortcuts, gives him a note for someone downstairs who can spare him the long wait at the pharmacy.

After Dr. Truman comes back, a family from the other hospital arrives. The parents and young girl are shy and nervous. It was bad enough having to get used to the other clinic. Losing that and having to start all over again is almost the last straw. They are surprised to be met at the door by the doctor. They knew he was famous and they had thought he would be grand. He shows them around. They begin to relax and ask questions. Sue makes coffee for everybody and they go into the office to talk.

After she has unhooked the thalassemia children, Monica sets up the baby of Michael and Mary for an infusion through the "Hickman line," the indwelling catheter that many of the children in intensive treatment wear in the subclavian vein under the right collarbone.

The baby is almost two but looks more like a year. She has no hair, but you can see that if she did, she would have the coloring of her mother, who is tiny and very young, with long straight red hair and a pale underwater face. She holds the baby on a pillow, and the child sleeps while the drug drips slowly in from the bottle on the pole.

Michael is with them, since he gave up his job when the child nearly died after a relapse, and so is Mary's brother, who takes time off from work to be here, because it seems like his job to protect them all. *Mary Poppins* clamors on, unnoticed.

Cindy is typing letters and making phone calls to set up appointments. Sue makes the trek to the old wing of the hospital to visit her patients on Burnham 4 and talk to the nurses.

She spends time with a good-looking eighteen-year-old whose baldness makes him look intellectual, who is in for five days of continual infusion through the Hickman line. One of the drugs makes him vomit, and he gets mouth sores. "I've learned to live with it." He has to miss a few days of school each month, but he will graduate soon with his class.

"Going to the prom?"

"Got nobody to take. Some of the girls I used to know are sort of scared of me now."

Elena, who is the same age, has rhabdomyosarcoma, a cancer that started as a lump on her wrist and would have spread very fast if not operated on and treated. For two years, she has to be in the hospital for four days every month. She gets very sick, so she hibernates in bed with the covers up to her pointed chin, doing nothing, talking to no one, eating nothing, losing five pounds each time, surfacing occasionally to throw up delicately into the bowl by the bed.

Some of her friends have dropped away, but the ones who stayed are hers for life. Her philosophy about the ordeal is that it has made her a better person and taught her to think more of others than of herself.

When she was quite young, she had a premonition that she would be very sick. Her family has had a lot of cancer, and four months ago her mother, to whom she was very close, died of it. Hibernating, Elena dreams of her mother and believes that she will grieve for her all her life. The one friend she made on the ward last year was a boy who had lost his father while he was in treatment. A few weeks ago this boy relapsed and died. Elena, who is very quiet and controlled and private, does not try to make friends with any of the other patients now.

Sue goes back to the clinic and removes the IV from Mary's baby and carefully cleans and tapes up the end of the catheter. Mary and Michael and the protective brother leave. Adele from Social Services, who takes care of the clinic's patients who need help in coping, comes up for tea. So does an English woman doctor from Radiation, bringing a cake.

The phone rings. Cindy has gone home. Dr. Truman answers.

"All right . . . yes . . . of course it's no bother. Bring her in tomorrow."

Chapter FIVE 🌿

*F*or parents and their children who have to go through the long grueling outpatient treatment, the hematology clinic becomes the focus of their lives.

Deborah was not the only mother who felt that she had lost contact with her former world because of her child's leukemia.

Having a child with cancer is something like being bereaved. People don't know what to say to you. They avoid you. They don't know if it's all right to talk about it. They are afraid of you, although what they really are afraid of is their own inability to help.

If only they would simply go to you, as soon as possible after they hear the news, and just put their arms around you without saying anything, if they don't know what to say. . . .

Parents of critically ill children know all the things that people say—and don't say; what they do—and fail to do.

When Lily's son's brain tumor killed him before he ever made it to college, the repressed New England side of the family never came, even from only a short distance away. They weren't up to it. They never wrote. They never spoke of it. They were "at a loss" to speak about the loss.

Clara's emotional family could speak about Maria's leukemia, but only in terms of themselves: *I can't deal with this. . . . I don't know what to do. . . . My granddaughter! . . . I can't be any help to Clara. I'm too sensitive to other people's pain.*

The mothers find themselves landed with the extra burden of having to make it easier for other people, jockeying along an awkward phone conversation, making the first move to show, "It's all right, you can ask me about it," protecting people who ought to be protecting them.

Laura learned that there were people to whom she had better say tumor, not cancer. Her daughter Krissie's good brash way was to tell everyone she had bone cancer and offer to take off her artificial leg for them if they wanted, rather than see them look at her below the hips, and then not look.

After Caryn got sick and bald and green, Jerri and Ed began to drive ten miles to the next town to do their shopping, to avoid people they knew in the local supermarket, who tried to avoid them in the aisles.

Also in a supermarket—one of the unlikely places where the dramas of life are staged—Deborah had David and the baby in a shopping cart. David was bald, as he was during much of his three years of chemotherapy. It was too hot to wear a cap, and like almost all the children, he had stopped minding about his hair.

Deborah, like most of the mothers, still did mind. When a nice old lady stopped by with a benevolent smile and cooed, "Isn't it funny that your baby has more hair than your older boy?" Deborah flashed out at her, "No, lady, because my baby doesn't have cancer."

The nice old lady's mauve smile faded into her ashen face, and Deborah was consumed with that ever-ready guilt, mixed with anger at herself for being still so vulnerable, and some anger at the old lady for making her feel guilty.

At the large corporation where he worked, Mark, the father of a son in treatment with Dr. Truman, saw friends taking new routes through his department to avoid passing by his desk and carrying their trays to another table in the cafeteria. At the same time, several strangers and people he hardly knew sought him out to talk about his sick child and to tell him that they had tangled with cancer and won, and that he should never give up hope.

They were a much greater support than the friends at home who knew all about cancer in theory and who told his wife she was doing it all wrong.

"You should have gone to this doctor I know. He's the only man in town."

"Radiation? No one's doing that anymore."

"Call Saint Jude's in Memphis. It's the only place."

"Why mess with Mass. General? Children's is the only place."

If she had been going to Children's Hospital, they would have asked her, "Why not Mass. General?"

"Why are you smiling?" a friend asked Judy, surprised to meet her at the cleaner's, as if it were not worth dry cleaning clothes when your boy was in the hospital having gangrene cleaned out of his legs.

"Why not?" Judy asked, still smiling, because her face is made like that.

"But I was going to say—I've been wanting to call you, but I didn't know what to say. I wanted to say I'm so sorry about Christopher, but you look as if you don't want to talk about it."

"What else would I talk about?" Judy beamed.

But not everybody wants to hear. Jerri's mother would grab her arm and ask, "How's Caryn?" searching her face with troubled eyes, but when Jerri started to share her own anxiety, her mother was already off into the saga of her own problems.

"It's terrible to be old and lonely. Nobody cares. 'How are you doing?' they say, and then walk on. Everybody wants to know, but nobody wants to listen."

You can say that again, Jerri said to herself.

68

And so do I. When I was starting The Samaritans, a suicide prevention service in Boston, people at parties would invite me to "tell me *all* about The Samaritans and what you do for suicidal people."

At first, I started to tell them, until I realized that they didn't want to know. All they wanted was to have asked. *There, I've shown interest, but what's she carrying on about? Gone a bit fanatic. I didn't ask for a sermon.*

In the fifteen years that I have worked with The Samaritans, I have talked to many people who have lost someone through suicide and heard how they and their families were shunned afterward as if they were unclean. Suicide, even more than cancer, is still a taboo subject to many people, too shameful to be voiced. The unhappy person who has taken his or her own life becomes unspeakable. The family is avoided, partly because no one knows what to say to them, partly because it must be in some way their fault. Scapegoating, finding a culprit, is one of the worst things people do to survivors after a suicide, who feel hideously guilty anyway without any outside help.

Even parents of leukemia children sometimes get blamed, obliquely if not to their faces, by the guessers and gossips who must find some reason, rather than face the idea that they could be next in line for the random assailant.

The mothers remember the thoughtless, clumsy people, but they remember the marvelous people more clearly: the old couple next door who take over the baby while the sick child is in the hospital. The sister with four children who brings food without being asked and comes fifty miles to clean your house. The neighbors who have left supper on the doorstep when you get back late from the hospital. The friends who go with you to the clinic or take your child there for treatment when you have the flu. The grandfather who realizes that the other children are desperate for attention. The grandmother who brings eighteen silly little wrapped packages to the children's ward marked

OPEN AT 4:15 ON WEDNESDAY OR DON'T LOOK AT THIS TILL 8:45 THURSDAY.

Vast, expensive, inappropriate presents don't help anyone, except perhaps the giver, who wants helplessly to *do* something. Small children can get spoiled and uppity and start lording it in the hospital bed and ordering their parents about. Older children look aghast at the loot they hardly have the energy to unwrap.

Krissie gave a lot of it to her younger sister, who had been quite naturally jealous.

"Why do they send me all this? Do they think I'm just a poor little sick kid?"

What she did want were the yellow ribbons on the trees all down her street when she came home after the amputation, and the painted sheet hung between the lamp posts that said WELCOME HOME KRISSIE, as if she were an Olympic gold medalist.

At junior high graduation soon after, the knee mechanism of her new leg was broken, so when her name was called for a prize for which she had studied at home, she stood up with a long skirt over her one leg and a big straw hat on her bald skull, and hundreds of parents and students jumped up and cheered her for being alive.

Janet will never forget Paul's last summer. His bone marrow was not holding its own. He had very little time left, so they rented a cottage on Cape Cod, which he loved.

Being on prednisone, he was always hungry. Ill as he was, he loved to eat. A local steak restaurant was his Elysium (the family still makes a pilgrimage there on his birthday), and steak his golden fleece.

The first evening, outside the next-door cottage, a retired policeman called Tony was cooking steak. Paul smelled the evocative, stinging, meaty smoke of it and wandered over to look. Eleanor came out with plates and knives and forks for the picnic table. Paul didn't exactly beg like a dog, but he let it be known that he would love a piece of steak.

70

The next day Janet told them why Paul was on Cape Cod. That whole week, Tony and Eleanor fed Paul extra meals. Eleanor took him shell hunting and Tony took him fishing. Janet suspended anxiety and actually slept in the daytime and read books. Paul cast off his prednisone moodiness to fall in love with his neighbors. He left for home wearing Tony's police badge.

Diane's best memory of kindness was from the mother of a little boy who had shared a hospital room with Kevin after they had both relapsed from the same type of leukemia.

Kevin regained remission and was discharged. Diane heard later that Timmy had died.

When Diane called, Timmy's mother asked her, "Do you remember when our boys were in that room together, and Dr. Truman told us they had a fifty-fifty chance? Timmy was the half that didn't make it, and Kevin was the half that did."

"Why Kevin and not Timmy? I don't understand. It's not fair that he had to go through all that for nothing!" Diane was crying, although Timmy's mother was calm. "It almost makes me want to back off and pull Kevin out of chemo. It's not worth it."

"But it's Kevin who makes it worth it, Diane, for me as well as you. The survivors are what make it all worthwhile."

Diane had called to comfort her, and she ended up comforting Diane.

Parents need all the support they can get, both inside and outside the hospital. In most of the places where seriously ill children are treated, psychiatrists and counselors and group meetings are available for the families.

Dr. Selter, the psychiatrist who sees many of Dr. Truman's families at least once, finds that one of the most common difficulties is that women need to have people around them to talk to, while men tend to get more withdrawn in this kind of crisis.

Many parents need to search for a reason, something or someone on whom to dump their angry frustration at what has happened to their child. The doctor's job is to listen to that, sometimes to let them be angry with him, if that helps, and to reintroduce the element of hope. Sometimes, as with the women at Ronald McDonald House and Rest Inn Retreat, a mother just needs to be able to say "I can't do any more" to someone who can tell her "That's all right. It is terrible" and simply bear witness to the pain, so that she can take a breath and go on again.

Some of the parents would never talk to a psychiatrist or a counselor because their family creed has always been, "You deal with your own troubles," or, "Only crazy people go to shrinks." They are leery of the whole therapy scene and afraid that if they were to ask someone for help, it would be like admitting, "There's something wrong with me."

In actual fact, it's the other way around. Recognizing that you need help is intelligent. Taking the always difficult step of asking for it is a sign of strength, not weakness.

Adele, a social worker at Mass. General, who is quiet and sensible, with the humorous outlook without which one is lost in her trade, often finds no response to her initial low-key approach.

At the beginning of the illness, the parents are too shocked and confused to think of anything else except their child. They don't want to be bothered with anything. Some are reeling; they can hardly talk. Nothing anyone could offer could be good enough at a time like this except to be told that the diagnosis was wrong.

So Adele hangs around, turning up in the ward or the clinic as if by chance, getting to know them a little better each time, ready to move in if there is some practical difficulty she can sort out for them. Sometimes it's money. Sometimes it's the difficulty of getting a child to the hospital for treatment. Sometimes it's a tragic history of so much gone wrong already, illness, a broken home or no home, the loss of another child, drugs, alcohol, a father in jail.

When children are in the hospital, many people are there for them. Adele's function, as she sees it, is to be the one who is there for the parents. Not formally—they are usually too busy with the child to make appointments—but Adele will just happen to be there, following them along, no big deal, an outlet for emotions, someone to talk to if anyone feels like talking.

At one time, she had an open support group going in the hospital, but it didn't work out. It was impossible to find a time that would suit everyone. The meetings had to be open so that people could wander in and out, and so the strength of the group's trust and commitment never developed. People were at different stages of experience. Some were too devastated to talk or listen. Some had heard too much already. Some were still so shackled with guilt about having a sick child that they didn't feel they deserved support or help and wouldn't come to the group to unload or learn how others coped.

Adele brooded, *Where did I go wrong?* It was obvious the group wasn't going to work while the parents were on the ward or in the clinic, so she started an evening group, where parents come independently. The meetings are at the hospital, because that's central for everyone. They are closed sessions for which ten or fifteen people are signed up for several weeks. The group is partly educational, which gives everyone the benefit of understanding more about the illness as well as getting the emotional support they need.

Dr. Truman or Sue or Monica or another doctor or oncology nurse comes to speak and answer questions, and when they leave, the talking and sharing and support starts by itself. Adele is there protectively, to referee if someone tries to hog the time and not let anyone else get a word in edgewise, a familiar hazard in any group, known to social workers as "overtalking."

The benefits are obvious. Since everyone else there has been through the same mill, it's a safe place to talk about fears, weakness, guilt, resentment, rage, and loss of hope. Veterans can succor newcomers, who can see: *You did it. You survived. You look all right. Your family didn't go under.* Hope rekindles.

Shy people learn to make friends. They may be afraid to talk at first. *No one must know me. My problem is too big, or too small, compared with theirs. I feel dumb. They'll think I'm stupid. Better keep my mouth shut.* Usually by the third meeting, they've begun to talk.

More men are coming now that the group is called educational. They don't want any part of "feelings," so they'll come just for the information. And then they stay, and come out with a load of sorrow and outrage, and perhaps find themselves able really to talk honestly with their wives for the first time.

Almost all the parents get some help and solace from the groups, and a feeling of belonging to a fellowship that can do more than anything to nourish the ego. Some don't like it that John or Sue or Monica gets kicked out before the talking part. They would prefer them to stay, although there are undoubtedly some who might not tell the toughest things if they were there, since they have to see them next week in the clinic.

Some parents say the sessions are too expensive. One or two told me that they dropped out because they felt they were being studied, which is certainly not the way Adele intends it, and it's a pity that it seems that way to them.

However, for those who don't want a professional presence, even if it's only a protective referee for overtalking, there are self-help nonprofessional groups where you pay for nothing except the cookies and tea bags when it's your turn.

There are large organizations like Candlelighters and The Compassionate Friends* that have national centers for information and guidance, and branches all over the country. Candlelighters is for parents of children with cancer. They provide communication between parents and medical professionals, and guidelines for starting small local groups, who can then run their own show any way they want.

The Compassionate Friends promote self-help groups for parents who have lost a child and for the surviving brothers and sisters. Members sometimes stay on in their groups for years after the child died, to be able to help new members along the slow, ancient road of grief where they themselves have traveled and reached the end in peace.

Small spontaneous groups also spring up without sponsorship, and these can be very close and loving and valuable—just a group of people who need each other—although it's more difficult to keep them going without some kind of organization behind you. They are started out of initial enthusiasm and need among the parents at a particular hospital. New people come in, but as the older ones gradually drop out because their child is well, or because their child has died and they feel like a skeleton at the feast among those who are talking about living children, it is hard to find enough leaders to carry it along.

Sandy had five children under six when her daughter Jane got leukemia. She started a parents' group with another mother in Concord, northwest of Boston. Jane was in remission and doing all right on chemotherapy. Sandy's husband wouldn't talk about it, and she felt she needed more support than Jane did.

She was suffering from the guilt of the mother who knows she is supposed to be the protector. *What did I do*

*The Candlelighters Foundation, Suite 1011, 2025 Eye Street, N.W., Washington, D.C. 20006; The Compassionate Friends, P.O. Box 1347, Oakbrook, Illinois, 60521.

wrong? What didn't I do right? It helped her to be able to talk that out to people in the same situation and realize she wasn't the only sufferer, and be reminded that there is no one cause for leukemia, and none of the causes is the mother's fault.

When Jane relapsed, Sandy saw that the child needed support too, to cope with the disappointment and unfairness of it, after all those years of having to fill herself with toxic drugs. Dr. Truman told them of his other young patients in and around Concord, so that they could help each other. A local hospital gave them a room. Five teens came to the first meeting. A local doctor came and was rejected coldly for announcing that this group ought to be run by professionals. The mothers were there too, which was also a mistake. The teens clammed up.

So they asked the hospital for two rooms and had the parents' group in one and their children in the other. A social worker came to show a videotape of an interview with a leukemia child. After another meeting, the teen-agers froze out the social worker for making rules and for picking their brains.

"He's studying for a degree," Jane said, "and we think he's going to make cases of us."

The children's group went on by itself successfully. They could talk honestly and really help each other with things like gaining weight and losing hair. A new girl who still had hers swore, "I'd rather die than lose my hair. A wig— gross!"

Someone else said quietly, "How do *I* look?"

"Fine. But then you've still got—"

The other girl took off her wig, grinning.

As the children's group grew and more younger children came, the adult group merged into it, because the mothers needed to be at the meetings with the younger ones. When she regained remission and was stabilized, Jane would tell the others, "Look at me. I relapsed, and I'm not dead. You're not going to die. Let's show thanks, not fear."

Jane is in college now and Sandy doesn't need the group, but she still goes to the monthly meetings because she isn't sure they would go on without her. Parents whose children are sick can't always come. The older children sometimes say, as Jane used to, "I don't want to go. I don't want to think about my cancer." But everyone goes when they know about someone who is having a very hard time and needs special help.

Sometimes Sandy takes the coffee and cakes and information pamphlets and goes to the room and sits there alone. She doesn't mind. If someone came, she'd be there for them.

The group still means a tremendous lot to her because it represents her salvation. Out of her own predicament, she created something that has helped dozens of other people.

"How can something so devastating become so wonderful?"

Her pride in that has helped to make her feel that her life is worthwhile.

At the lowest ebb, when she lost hope for Jane, she was going to kill herself.

"What stopped you?"

"I thought about all these children and how hard they fought to keep their lives. I couldn't throw mine away."

Chapter S I X 🌰

"*T*he disease settled into our house, is what it did," one mother told me. "Leukemia became part of our lives, and our lives part of *it*. Where did those two years go? I've written them off."

The long day-to-day, week-by-week drag of treatment absorbs your life. The clinic becomes like a second home, except that it's a home you don't want to have to go to. John Truman, Sue, Monica, and Cindy have become close friends, and temporarily the most important people in your life; but they are friends you would rather not have had to make.

The endless clinic visits, the blood tests, the increasing difficulty of finding a good vein for the intravenous drugs, the fear and pain of a lumbar puncture—the mother's ordeal can be almost as bad as the child's because she must subject him or her to it and stand by, unable to bear the pain for the child herself.

When Ann's little boy had to go for radiation, she looked at the grown-ups waiting in the radiation unit and was jealous of them.

"I thought they were lucky. Crazy! But that's how I was. They had cancer, but they had it themselves. I had to see my child have it and not be able to have it for him."

In the clinic, it still hurts to see so many sick children, and the sickest are the ones you see most. When they are not there, you are afraid to ask, because you know what it might mean. Some parents talk to each other in the waiting room or the treatment room. Some only talk to the staff or to their own child, wrapped in their own anxiety, waiting for test results, white cell and bone marrow counts, hemoglobin levels, the numbers around which life revolves. Here, as on the wards, it depends on what you are like in the real—or unreal—world outside.

That's true of every aspect of a child's illness. Tiresome children don't become angelic. Good children don't turn into monsters, except under the temporary effect of drugs like prednisone, known to its victims as "ugly pills." A teenager who was aggressive and moody before probably goes back to that when shock and fear have quieted into the routine of treatment. An emotional father who cries easily is going to weep for his child with cancer. A terse, secret man is not going to become emotionally articulate now. An energetic, efficient mother will have the family organized and all the treatment down on charts and calendars. A dreamy, disordered mother won't suddenly start making the beds after breakfast and throwing out moldy little dishes from the back of the refrigerator, and if she writes things down, it is because, with the confusion of information coming at her, she knows that she will, as usual, forget.

Intensive research is going on all over the world to develop a cure for leukemia, but until it materializes, chemotherapy is the most effective treatment, at the cost of varying side effects for the child, which can sometimes be worse than the illness.

Some children are lucky enough to avoid the vomiting that follows each dose of the stronger drugs, but almost everyone loses some or all of their hair. They hate that, but they accept it. Some of the mothers mind it more than their children do.

Nine-year-old Paddy comes galloping through the house from the school bus, slings her book bag in one corner, her jacket in another, her dark curly hair into a half-open drawer in the kitchen, and jumps out bald into the garden where her friend from next door is waiting.

"Is that the thing you told me cost four hundred dollars?"

I ask her mother. The wig hangs out of the drawer and a cat reaches gracefully up to pull it down to the floor.

"She's never worn that one. This is a nylon one the department store gives free to leukemia children."

One of the shocks of chemotherapy is the price of wigs and how awful they can be. When Caryn pulled out the first tufts of her beautiful long brown hair in the car going home from the hospital, her mother had to stop off the road, so that they could cry together. As it thinned, her father cut it short, since Jerri could not bear to, and when they saw the "beautiful" styled human-hair wigs in the salon near the hospital, they cried again, not only about the prices, but because the wigs were so hideously unlike Caryn, whose thick brown Indian squaw hair was now almost all gone.

Another shock is how much you mind the loss of your child's hair, even though you are facing the possible loss of a life. To compensate, you spend the three or four hundred dollars, glad to be able to do *something,* and the child wears the wig self-consciously for a while, until it ends up in the costume box, to be worn at Halloween.

Kim and Jill think now that they will want a wig, but they may end up like most of the other children and teenagers who prefer to wear woolen caps or three-cornered kerchiefs. Sometimes nothing at all, in defiance of the stares, or worse still, the grown-up stare and the quickly averted eyes that the bald head attracts, curiously small and narrow on a grown body.

Their contemporaries usually handle it better.

"Though a few jerks at school gave me a hard time at first," Chris said.

"Why? Because they didn't understand?"

"Because they're jerks. I pulverized 'em. Now I like myself either way, with or without the wig. Some of the girls can't stand to see my skull. So I go 'Hullo dere!' " He lifts the blond wig like a cap. "They freak out."

Among the young ones, any teasing or snickers at school

soon stop when teachers explain about the illness and its treatment—which they should have done before the child came back to school. When I went to see seven-year-old Megan after her bone marrow transplant, I found her sitting on the floor in front of a dollhouse, her red calico kerchief falling low over her eyes as she was absorbed in pinning up scraps of curtains, the bare knobs at the base of her skull white under the raised back corner of the kerchief. Her friend, who was sticking up postage stamps for pictures, had masses of creamy blond hair that foamed out all around the kerchief, which she always wore in this house, to be like Megan.

After remission and during the months and years of treatment and tests, it is important that the child live as normal a life as possible. Parents who are still trying to absorb the significance of the news that the remission is holding and death has retreated are often shocked to hear Dr. Truman say, "Get her back to school. Sooner the better."

"But she's been so sick."

"Don't make an invalid out of her. Get her back into school, back into family life. Watch her like a hawk, but don't baby her. This is where your job really starts."

So you try not to let fears from the recent past carry you into fear of the future. You live in the present. That's your best hope.

If you have a child with bone cancer like Krissie, you don't think much about last year's tall, healthy little girl with two legs who did everything like everyone else before the vague pains in the thigh started, nor about the time next year, the year after, when she may not be alive if the cancer metastasizes again. You think about watching from the window her bony, wasted figure on the stork legs, one hers, one not, with a wool hat jammed down over her wig, waiting in the frozen dawn for the school bus in January, because the best hope—for now—is for her to live like everyone else.

Her mother Laura says, "It wasn't hard for Krissie to go back to school after all those months before and after the operation. All her friends had come to see her at the hospital and at home. The whole school knew. They were marvelous. They accepted it more easily than some of the grown-ups in my family. She comes home from school with friends—coat off, wig off, boots off, leg off. The hardest thing now is going back to the hospital on her clinic day, because it's a reminder that she's sick."

You have to balance between overprotecting and taking risks. Laura and Tom let Krissie go to Egypt for a week with a school group. She was tired and ill after she got home, but the trip was the highlight of her life.

Not treating your child like an invalid doesn't mean relaxing the strict drug program or the regular tests. If there is a relapse, it's back into the hospital again, as quickly as possible. Schools and parents of your child's friends can learn to cooperate, to include the sick child without asking too much of her, and to warn you of other children's infections to which she is so vulnerable, with her immune system weakened by the cancer-killing drugs, especially that old archenemy, chicken pox.

Doctors like John Truman know that the parents and the rest of the family are a vital part of a child's treatment. But the parents are in a somewhat ambivalent position. They have a huge job to do, with the day-to-day care of their child, but the doctor is still in charge. If he is the right kind of doctor who pays attention to the family, he will listen to your ideas and observations. If he isn't, you will do well to find someone else.

Even with the right kind of doctor, there may be times when you don't agree with his decisions, but you may not have the confidence or courage to say so. Most doctors are more approachable than people think, if the approach is made not as an argument or a criticism but as a need for information. Doctors in this field expect and welcome questions. Ask questions first. Find out the facts on which the decision is based. Then say what you think.

If something is obviously wrong with the care of your child in the hospital, say what you think right away. You and your child have rights. If you don't know them, ask the Patient Advocate or someone from Social Services. You need to know, for instance, that a student or an intern is allowed two tries to get into a vein, no more. After that, you can insist that a doctor do it.

Most of the staff will be wonderful, but you may have the bad luck to run into one of the few who shouldn't be in the business.

When Brian's weight was down to sixty-five pounds and he could not eat because he was so ill with Hodgkin's and the drugs were so powerful and the radiation was burning ulcers in his stomach, a gastrointestinal specialist who did not know his months of courage told him superciliously, "You have to want to live, you know."

Brian's mother exercised her rights by chasing the fool out of the room and down the corridor.

When Janet's Paul was on the ward, there were too many hotshot interns coming in and out for his mother's liking. One of them said smoothly one day, "I guess you're terminal now, Paul." After that, Dr. Truman treated him as an outpatient in his clinic.

Mary Lou's daughter Nicole is blind. The day after surgery, she needed to pull on the cord that lights up the bed numbers in the nurses' station. The third or fourth time, the evening nurse came and stood in the doorway. Not seeing her, Nicole pulled the cord again.

"Can't you see I'm here?" the nurse asked angrily.

After she had gone, Nicole had to pull the cord again, perhaps hoping for another nurse, and the angry one stormed in and took away her light cord.

Nicole was terrified. Mary Lou was upset when she heard about it, but being a soft lady, she only complained mildly to the charge nurse and excused the evening nurse because she knew she didn't like that shift.

"Next time I'll do it differently," she says grimly. "I'll go to the supervisor, the head of the hospital, the board of trustees. . . ."

Hospitals give mothers books with information about diets during chemotherapy, and about how to keep a vomiting child nourished. They provide basic useful information about what foods to choose and what to avoid, how to lessen vomiting, supply enough calories and protein, and tempt the appetite of a tired child whose taste has been dulled by the chemicals, so that sweet, sour, bitter, salty, all taste equally unappetizing.

But many parents, especially those whose life-style includes health foods and natural substances and progressive ideas on nutrition, want to explore new theories about diet and cancer.

Macrobiotics? High-potency vitamins? Dr. Truman dismisses them as of no value at all and potentially dangerous. "Hypervitaminosis, especially with vitamin A, can cause a lot of trouble, like rashes and kidney stones. It verges on quackery, but parents go for it because it's one of the few things they can do, and unscrupulous people cash in on their misery. The macrobiotic stuff is very expensive. It's a rip-off. They claim miraculous cures. I claim it wasn't cancer in the first place."

Less controversial diets and exercises and health cures he will go along with, "as long as they do no harm and you don't stop the treatment."

However much parents trust their doctor, they aren't going to let any chance go by without trying everything. As long as the diets and vitamins and massage and exercises aren't harmful, they shouldn't be put off by lack of encouragement or be intimidated by the hospital and the whole medical mystique. If you powerfully believe that this or that wholesome thing will help your child, perhaps it will.

Although John Truman is a bit skeptical about anything

that sounds like nature cures and health food fads, he is a hundred percent in favor of the instincts of parents. He listens. He picks up information from what mothers observe and understands that, although appearance and symptoms and tests may be normal, if a mother says, "I can't put my finger on it, but I just know this child is *sick*," he'd better look more closely.

Because parents are, after all, the experts. They very quickly become old hands. The names of all the complicated drugs roll, as Dr. Truman told Deborah they would, off their tongues like everyday words. They learn to talk in percentages, like the doctors.

"A ninety-five percent chance of remission."

When the disease is diagnosed, the doctor will usually give parents a percentage, although to the child he is more likely to say, "You have leukemia, but we know how to treat it."

The percentages that doctors give and that parents remember and repeat like talismans, are pretty accurate. They are based on past and current information fed by about thirty treatment clinics throughout the country into the computers of cancer research centers. Doctors use percentages a lot, to make complicated medical data more understandable and to pin down an elusive situation and give people something to hang on to.

If parents hear, "Your child has an eighty percent chance of remission," they see the figure 80, not the figure 20. That is an intrepid quality that all but the most defeatist of parents share. If told, "Your child has a fifty-fifty chance," they see the top 50, upward toward life. The bottle is not half empty, it is half full.

Even if things get so bad that the doctor has to tell a mother, "We've only got a five percent chance of winning," the number 95 does not appear on the screen of her mind. She is looking at the 5.

One chance in a hundred? All right, we'll be that one.

Chapter SEVEN 🌿

"**Y**ou can beat the odds," Bert always thought. "If you know how to operate, you can always beat the odds."

When he was a skinny little boy, stifling bouts of asthma often kept him watching from a window while other boys scuffled and shrieked and hurled each other to the ground. He grew out of it to be a tall young man, broad and athletic. He learned to believe that you can beat anything, and he always proved himself right. When he broke his back in a skiing accident in Austria, he might have remained paralyzed, but after risking a life-or-death operation, he beat those shivery odds, without surprise.

"I knew I could, so I did. That's how it works."

He married a small girl with dark blond hair and a sweet, sad smile who would have married him anyway, paralyzed or not. His business was successful. He and Tobey prospered and bought a house in one of the old towns south of Boston.

No children? Possibly the result of the spine fracture, but that could be taken care of too. Unlike many men who wrestle with a prejudice against "another man's child," Bert was as eager to adopt as Tobey was.

Confidently, they applied to an agency, a handsome young couple, loving and generous, well placed to be the best kind of parents. It was a surprise to learn that their chances of adopting a white child who was healthy in mind and body were very small.

They were victims of the barren parents' baffling paradox: People keep on having babies they don't want, but those who want them can't get them. They considered the odds: very low, but so were the odds on the broken back. Another challenge here to beat.

After a long wait they were invited to a meeting with other prospective parents. At the end of the meeting, which was not encouraging, everybody got up and left. *Improve the odds, Bert.* While the others traipsed out, wistful and depressed, he bounced up and shook the speaker's hand and thanked him in a way that Tobey, who was used to listening while Bert talked, was afraid was too confident, but that Bert hoped would sweep the agency man into his own optimism and make things happen.

After that, the other couples continued to wait obediently, wondering whether they would be too old to manage a baby by the time they got one. Bert wrote or telephoned the agency once or twice a week.

"If a baby does turn up, I want them to think of us as sitting on their doorstep. 'Here you are.' 'Thank you.' "

Bert was in business with a friend, producing and marketing cheeses from factories in Wisconsin. He was off in Minnesota, buying milk or selling cheese. Tobey was at home oiling their bicycles because they were going to spend July riding up and down some New England mountains. The phone rang. She came in from the garage.

"Oh. When? . . . Tomorrow. Thank you."

She called Bert in Minneapolis. "Come home. We're adopting a child."

His name was Charley. He was three months old, the healthy, beautiful, cheery baby on whom the odds had been so low. On the way home from the agency, they stopped to buy a crib and a box of disposable diapers, and read the directions on the box to find out how to put them on.

They knew nothing about the baby's first parents except height and weight and that the young mother had never told anybody who the father was. They did not need to know more. Charley was their child and an utter delight from the start, not strange with them, a gorgeous child with fine gold hair, full cheeks, and a laughing face. Everybody loved him. He was the star of the neighborhood, doted upon by teenage babysitters, other children's grandmothers, Bert and Tobey's friends and families, and the new friends that Tobey made among the local mothers, now that she was in their club.

At about nine months, they took Charley to the courthouse to sign the final adoption papers. Wanting the judge to see that they were the finest parents of the finest boy, it was disappointing that Charley had a messy cold and that he had got himself bruised in so many places.

"They'll think we're child beaters," Tobey laughed, but she could not understand why, although she was gentle, he would bruise so easily while she was dressing him or picking him up out of the bath.

The cold became a fever that went up and down for several weeks. Tobey took him to their pediatrician or one of his partners half a dozen times, but the fever did not respond to the antibiotics and aspirin they prescribed. He was uncomfortable. He flung himself about. He woke and cried at night and would not settle down. When Bert came back from a business trip, the baby seemed very ill, restless, his stomach swollen, although he was not eating much, and there were still the bruises and a rash of little red marks.

"The doctors just keep saying to continue the aspirin." Carrying the sick child, Tobey looked doubtfully across the top of the silky yellow head.

Bert called the doctor. "I'm getting tired of this."

"Keep on with the aspirin. Bring him in tomorrow if he's fussy."

"Fussy!" Bert hung up the phone and turned to Tobey and the baby. "The hell with this. We're going to Mass. General."

The resident who examined Charley in the Emergency

88

Room called down the doctor who was Dr. Truman's associate.

"Your son has leukemia."

Bert had been standing. He sat down because his knees collapsed. He looked at Tobey. Her face over the silken head was numb, expressionless.

"Someone read a slide wrong": Bert's way of saying "This can't happen to us."

Dr. Fosburg shook his head. "His white cell count is a hundred and eighty thousand. That's very high. We have several tough days ahead of us."

"What—what are the odds?" So that we can beat them.

"I can't give you odds right now. He has a good chance, but this week will be bad, because he's been sick so long. A high white count gives you a lower prognosis than a low count at the start, and a child under two, especially a boy, is at greater risk than an older child."

That week in Intensive Care, full of tubes and needles and surrounded by nurses and monitoring machines, Charley almost died. He was miserable and in pain. The only thing that quieted him was being held by Tobey, hour after hour, under the bottles that dripped in the medication.

"Because he wasn't diagnosed for so long," Bert agonized to Dr. Fosburg, "because that bastard didn't do a blood test—does that lower the odds on his chances?"

"Not in the long run. The white counts would have been high anyway, but if he'd come to us earlier, he wouldn't have had to go through this hell."

"I'm right then, aren't I, to be furious with that doctor?"

Dr. Fosburg looked at him soberly. "I'd be bullshit."

In contrast to Dr. Truman with his neat good suits and white shirts and doctorly ties, Dr. Fosburg was a long-haired doctor with a Mexican moustache who loped about the hospital in jeans and plaid shirts and a woodsman's waistcoat, much admired by his teenage patients and hardly ever away from his job.

One Saturday evening, he stayed less time than usual with Bert and Tobey, because he was going out. Watching Charley sleep in his tangle of tubing, they happily imagined the young doctor having dinner in an intimate little restaurant opposite a dear girl with a lot of soft loose hair, who would wear a long cotton skirt and ballet slippers and a white peasant blouse off her shoulders. She would talk lovingly and hold out her slender hand across the tablecloth—it would be an Italian restaurant with a checkered cloth and a wine bottle in straw—and she would be good to him.

When they were leaving to go home for their few hours sleep, Bert and Tobey met Dr. Fosburg in the hospital lobby, pushing a trolley stacked with boxes.

"Where have you been?"

"Late night at the discount house." He grinned through the moustache as happily as if he really had been with the girl in ballet slippers. "Buying some toys for the clinic."

Bert went through elaborate fantasies of what he might do and say to the pediatrician, although he did not plan to see him again. To his surprise, the man walked through the door of the Intensive Care Unit, spoke to a nurse, and came over to their alcove.

Concern for Charley? Apologies?

"I want you to remember," the doctor said defensively, "that I didn't see Charley myself last week. And the last time I saw him was just for the ear infection. That's all you brought him in for. Remember that."

Bert said nothing. Tobey looked at the doctor over the baby's burning head.

The day Charley was on the edge of death, trying to slip over, the pediatrician came back again. He had brought Charley's records.

"I want to make sure that the doctors here understand that I didn't see the child myself the week he came in here."

"No," Bert said. "Only the week before, and the week before that, when I know now he had all the symptoms of leukemia, and you—"

"No need to shout." The doctor looked nervously around the unit, where the priestess nurses on silent white rubber feet tended the small bodies and the machines that kept them alive.

"Get out." Bert dropped his voice and moved forward pugnaciously. "Get out of our lives."

They did not see him again, except for a chance encounter in the hospital parking lot, when Tobey was taking Charley back to the clinic for tests after he had been discharged.

"How is he?"

"Better," Tobey said grimly, proud of herself for not adding something childish like, "no thanks to you."

"Good. Now we shall have to see about finding you a psychiatrist, young lady."

At home, they had left Charley's high chair by the kitchen table with some colored relics of kiddie cereal from his last unwanted meal on the tray and his toys all over the house, as if he were sure to come home.

When he did come home, the doctors were optimistic, especially Dr. Fosburg, who tended to be hopeful about odds, like Bert, while Dr. Truman preferred to tell you straight out all the worst things, which then often turned out to be better than you expected. Friends and neighbors, who had done all the right things during the week of hell, like feeding the dog, cleaning, bringing food, and coming to the hospital, flocked to the house to see the miracle boy.

He smiled for them, but not chubbily anymore. The full cheeks were narrower. Off the intravenous feeding, he was eating very little. He was still bruised, because the strength of the chemicals that had reduced the white cell count had also destroyed some of the platelets, the blood's clotting factor. The continuing treatment in the clinic was almost as bad as what he had already gone through—radiation, bone marrow samples, spinal taps, blood tests, pills that he vomited back up, intravenous drugs.

How could a child that size stand all this? Except when he was on prednisone, which makes any child as bloated and irritable as a gouty old man, Charley continued to be cheerful and loving, lurching toward you with open arms to be picked up, playing in the clinic with the toys Dr. Fosburg had bought that Saturday evening, scattering the contents of Cindy's lower desk drawer to find her peppermints.

Bert went back to his neglected business. Tobey's whole life was the treatment. She dreaded clinic days: holding him tightly for the assaults on his spine and blood vessels, watching them give the anesthetic to keep him motionless in the radiation room, waiting, waiting with the other tormented mothers for the results of the tests that would tell them when he was at last in remission.

"Come on, Charley, we're going in the car."

"Where going?" He was talking pretty well by now.

"See Cindy."

"Hokay."

A month after the diagnosis, he was in remission. There were cries of praise in the clinic, all staff and parents rejoicing, including a wan mother whose child would never be in remission again.

Remission is winning first prize, being top of the class, getting engaged to someone lovely, picking a winning number in the lottery. Everyone shares in the happiness, a public joy, at least in the small world of pediatric hematology.

For nearly eight months, the remission held. Charley was only going to the clinic once a month, with pills every day and the disagreeable prednisone every fourth month. Otherwise he was living the life of a healthy and strong three-year-old. He pushed the lawn mower, ran, climbed, fell, threw balls wildly, and made the usual ineffective sweeps at catching them.

"Looks like the healthiest kid in town," Bert and Tobey told each other.

When your child is in remission, you hold your luck like a thin-shelled egg, but you have to behave outwardly as if you believe the remission is permanent and the child will be well. Naturally you are careful, and you watch every small sign and pounce on anything wrong and stay away from people with colds; but you have to allow the child as normal a life as possible. Otherwise he will end up as neurotic as you will make yourself.

Tobey was never quite free of the worry. She was the one who kept the clinic dates on her calendar. Sometimes when she looked at Charley or touched him, she was pierced by the reminder that the blood that flowed under that tight smooth skin of this lovely child might be endangered again by cancer cells.

Bert's way, while Charley was well, was to deny the truth of the illness. He did not want to talk about it anymore. When he looked at Charley, he saw only a boy, a son with a future. Tobey saw him in the present. Bert saw him at school, at college, skiing, sailing, golden boy on the tennis court, beating his father at singles.

Watching Charley playing in the garden with his cousins who had come from New York for Passover, they saw that he had come through the winter as well as anyone. They heard him laughing all the time, hysterically when the older girls grabbed him and roughed him up, saw him chugging behind the bigger boys, calling "Wait for me!"

"He looks like you at that age," Bert's family said, and Tobey's family saw him as just like her when her hair was still light yellow, as families invariably do with adopted children, either forgetting that there is no physical link, or making a special point of creating one.

After the seder that night, all the children were tired. Charley was flushed and grumpy. Tobey took his temperature.

"A hundred, that's nothing," one of the mothers said. "Mine always go up after they've been excited. Oh, but—"

Bert and Tobey had always played down the leukemia, because they did not want the family to treat Charley differently, and they did not want the wailing members of it to wail.

When Charley woke crying at three in the morning, his fever was a hundred and three. If you have a leukemia child, you don't sponge him down and give him baby aspirin. You take him to the hospital.

The woman resident who saw him there told Tobey that the white cell count was up a bit, but she did not know much about leukemia. She thought it was all right to take Charley home. All the way back, Tobey fretted: *Why are we driving home? Why didn't I insist that she call one of Charley's doctors? I know more about leukemia than she does. Why am I such a rabbit?*

When she got home at six, Bert called Dr. Truman.

"It could be an infection of some kind." They waited. "I hate to make you turn around and come back in, but . . ." They waited. "It could be the enemy back at the gate."

That was the way he said it. "The enemy back at the gate." The invading barbarians. You thought they had slunk away routed, but it was only to regroup and rearm and come clamoring back, rattling spears and yelling for blood.

The sun was up, and the hospital had long been about its business: ambulances at the emergency entrance, police cars, the lobby already furnished with the people who sit in relays all day long, the bodies slumped in wheelchairs waiting to be pushed somewhere, the brisk morning army of staff pausing for a moment to buy from the newspaper man, who knows them all by name.

After the bone marrow sample had been taken, with more difficulty than usual, Bert and Tobey waited with Charley in the clinic, hardly speaking, their hearts like stones.

Dr. Truman came back shaking his head. The world opened up and dropped them off.

A relapse from remission when the child is no longer on chemotherapy is not the end. It is the beginning of more treatment. The news of a relapse during treatment is worse than the initial diagnosis. It means that the most effective drugs, those "best" drugs that are hurled into battle at first, are no longer destroying the cancer cells.

With each relapse, the treatment gets harder on the child. The drugs are more aggressive. The side effects are worse. Charley had to endure crushing doses of Methotrexate to try to get him back into remission for a bone marrow transplant—his only chance.

It's an old oncology cliché to say, with a rueful smile, that the treatment can be worse than the disease. Clichés are true, however, which is how they got to be clichés. You can explain to an older child why he has to be made so devastatingly sick and ask him to agree to the treatment. With a small child, you can't. You just have to do it to him without his permission.

Which is worse? For each family, it depends on the age of their child. Whatever that is, that is worst.

When Charley had struggled back into remission, still cheery, still trusting everybody, paddling happily ahead of Tobey out of the elevator and down the dreadfully familiar corridor to the clinic, it was time to talk about a transplant.

What are the odds? One in ten thousand of finding an unrelated donor with a compatible blood type and marrow cells. With a twin, the odds are best, at one in two. A brother or sister, one in four. The mother's marrow has less than a one in a thousand chance of being compatible.

Dr. Truman wrote through the adoption agency to Charley's first mother. He asked her if she would be willing to come for tests. She would not see Charley or his new parents. No one need know her name.

She did not answer for quite a long time. While they were waiting, Bert and Tobey took Charley off to Nantucket for a long weekend while he was well enough to enjoy it. This remission could not last as long as the first one.

Nantucket lies twenty miles off the south coast of Cape Cod, the remains of the terminal moraine of a glacier that formed the rocky spine of the sandy Cape and dumped a few boulders farther on to form the islands of Martha's Vineyard and Nantucket, edged with long sandy beaches and indented by perfect harbors.

In the spring, Nantucket is a flowering moor, with wild aromatic scents and soft sandy roads wandering through the long bright grass. The little town where the steamers berth still has its cobbled main street and the beautiful old square brick houses of the rich whaling captains. In the summer, it has thousands of tourists each day who ruin it for each other.

In early May, almost nobody is there, and you can still see the pure salty charm of the town and harbor. The sun flicks brilliant lights off the water. The white boats at anchor rock in the warm wind, with a fast musical clicking of shrouds against mast. Bert and Tobey walked out along the wharf, with Charley running ahead. An old lady in a man's sweater stopped and bent to him, as old ladies were apt to do, because of the face he had.

"Look at him." She straightened up again as he ran off with his arms out to a young brown seagull. "Not a care in the world."

When they got back to the hospital, they learned that Charley's first mother had said no.

"Why?"

"She's married. She has a new baby, a new life."

"But Charley—"

"She hasn't told her husband about him. 'Go away,' she said in effect, 'and leave me alone.'"

The only chance now was to find an unrelated donor. The Red Cross often types bone marrow when they test the blood of their millions of donors. They would not disclose any information because donors only give them permission to use platelet data, not the HLA typing, which stands for Human Lymphocyte Antigen, and which must match the recipient.

"But surely nobody . . . wouldn't anyone welcome the chance to save a child's life?"

"It's considered to be a violation of their civil rights."

Another of today's clichés, but more misused and open to question.

There was not much time left.

Bert improved the odds by finding a friend, an expert in medical data, who persuaded the Red Cross to let him run their blood information through a computer. It came up with three possible bone marrow matches. The Red Cross sent those donors a postcard asking, "Would you consent to have your HLA typing released?" Nobody answered. The three people had either died, moved away without a forwarding address, or thrown away the postcards.

Four months after this tenuous remission that put him on the Nantucket wharf without a care in the world, Charley relapsed again. There were no signs of the illness, but the blood tests showed that even if high dosage could get him back into remission, it would be a very short one, not more than six or eight weeks.

Bert had abandoned his business by now. If his partner could not manage, it would have to go down the drain. Nothing mattered but Charley. Bert called every center that had bone marrow data, and although Charley was a rare blood type, a possible donor was found, with only one anomaly. The person—man or woman—refused.

The mother, the three people who got the postcards, and now this neuter person. Easy to be shocked. But nobody has ever asked us to have bright red liquid bone marrow drawn from our pelvis or breastbone for an unknown child who might not survive the transplant anyway. Would we . . . ?

Beavering away, because the transplant was Charley's only hope and his father's single-minded grail, Bert found the Anthony Nolan Foundation in England, named after a child who had died. It had forty thousand names of people who actively desired to be donors and thus improve, rather than jeopardize, their civil rights to help their fellow man.

There were two possible matches, close enough to give a fifty-fifty chance of success. Charley's white cell count was good enough. The flight to London was booked. The last tests on his bone marrow were being run.

Now that the grail was found, Bert tried to catch up with some business before he left. The hospital called him at the office.

"Something looks strange in Charley's slides."

"Oh well, we'll have to—" Bert caught himself about to give his usual answer, "We'll have to deal with that," and stopped. He knew that they would never get to England.

Charley was back in the hospital, going rapidly downhill. More cancer cells were being made, and no new lymph cells. He slept most of the time, hardly talking when he was awake, whimpering when he had to be moved. There was not much that could be done except to keep him comfortable and disturb him as little as possible. The best thing any nurse could do for him was to be able to work among the tangle of intravenous lines to change the bottles and get everything running without waking him.

He would open his eyes for Bert and Tobey, or for his favorite friends, like the babysitter he loved best, who came to the hospital every day. Sometimes she was the only one who could get him to take a pill. Sometimes it was Tobey, sometimes Ann, his small nurse with the long Hawaiian hair and short rounded white arms. Sometimes it was only Joe, who took over from Ann, a gently speaking young man with a gingery beard and light brown eyes. Sometimes he would curl away from everybody and cry, "No, no."

Bert got through the days by bringing work from the office. Tobey concentrated on Charley's treatment, following the blood count figures, questioning Dr. Truman and the nurses, reading about new research on leukemia, wanting in some way to hang on to the control that was slipping away from them all.

She talked to Ann who, on this distressing ward where the parents need attention as well as the children, always found time to stop and talk, however busy she was. Tobey needed to talk through Charley's illness, ferreting out where she had gone wrong, what had been hopeful, what ought to have been done.

"Why did we take so long to doubt the pediatrician? Why does one have this stupid blind faith in doctors just because they're set up in practice in a brick medical building with a lot of good-looking nurses and X-ray machines and glossy brochures? Why didn't he do blood tests? Why, why, why?"

Ann had listened to other parents complaining about doctors, sometimes with reason, sometimes out of the need to find a scapegoat, someone to take the blame for a random catastrophe that seems to be nobody's fault.

"Sometimes I wonder," she said, "whether a local doctor perhaps doesn't *want* to look for that kind of diagnosis, especially if he has a small practice and doesn't often see things like sarcoma and leukemia. Everybody finds ways to deny. You told me that Bert went through a time when he didn't want to admit that Charley had cancer. Even Dr. Truman sometimes keeps himself going by being unrealistically hopeful. So is this a sort of denial—if we don't do the blood tests, he won't have it? I've caught myself thinking that way. If a child gets very sick and distressed from certain drugs, sometimes I don't want to take his temperature, because if it's up, I'm going to have to give that drug. Almost as if by taking the temperature, you're creating the problem."

There was a new and experimental drug that could be

tried. Its effect would be violent. It was a last chance, although even if it worked, it might give Charley only a few more weeks of life.

Ann thought again about denial. A few more weeks of life, perhaps eight or ten days—isn't that denying the truth that Charley is dying?

Nurses can't tell doctors what to do, and many doctors don't care much about what the nurses think. But when Dr. Truman had described this new drug to Ann, he looked at her carefully and said, "I see by your face you don't agree."

"No, I don't. I don't think he should be put through any more."

"Well . . . thanks." The doctor nodded. "I have to talk to the parents now. I'll consider what you said."

The status of nurses in America has not improved as much as people would like to think, especially in the great teaching and research hospitals. The last time Ann had given a doctor her definite opinion, she had been ignored.

She had an eighteen-year-old patient with spina bifida and chronic osteomyelitis. While she was in the hospital for one more of her many bone operations, her brother was killed on the road.

"Keep a stiff upper lip," her parents told her, because that was their way of coping. "Be strong."

One night she woke screaming. When Ann went in, she told her about the nightmare of slitting her throat. "The blood drained out and everybody just sat there. Nobody did anything. I died. That was when I woke."

"Had you been thinking about suicide?"

"Sometimes. Ann, I think I need help. When I started in college this year, I had such a hard time, I went to a counselor. My mother was furious. I'm not supposed to need help. I'm strong. She tells me I haven't accepted my spina bifida, but it's she who hasn't. I'm supposed to be the way she wants me to be, and I can't, I can't—"

Ann told the surgeon, "She'd like to see someone from psychiatry."

"Well, I don't know. Let's wait awhile and see how she does."

"Till she kills herself?"

"Oh, come. She's one of my best-adjusted patients."

"How can a doctor who spends ten minutes a day with her know her like I do, when I'm with her all the time?"

"Calm down. We'll wait."

Nothing more was done.

Many of the doctors do encourage the older children and their families to see a psychiatrist at least once, for a chance to sort out their feelings. But some doctors seem to be as insecure as this girl's mother. They feel they should be enough. "If there's something emotionally wrong with her, does that mean there's something wrong with me?"

"This drug is new and very expensive. It can increase his vomiting. It can cause him pain. It's possibly lethal."

Dr. Truman asked Ann to be with them when he talked to Bert and Tobey. Nobody spoke for a while. Tobey let her hair fall forward and looked at the floor. Dr. Truman folded his clean hands. Ann looked out the window at the mass of cars trying to beat the rush hour, already jammed up on the highway that cuts the old Beacon Hill houses off from the river that used to run at the end of their gardens. Bert cleared his throat.

"What are the —"

"At best, perhaps a ten percent chance. We don't really know."

"I think we should take it," Bert said quickly, and Tobey looked up at him. Dr. Truman did not say anything.

"Is it fair," Tobey asked, "to hurt him more, when it might not even work?"

"It's all we have."

"How long would he take it?"

"Five days. It's an experimental drug, so Charley would have to be part of the study."

"Oh."

"The father part of me can feel like you do," the doctor

said carefully. "The scientist part is different. And I have to be your doctor. I'm no use to you as just another father."

"But if it was your child?"

He shook his head. "But it's yours, and you want to give him every chance. So do I."

"You want to go ahead?" Bert asked.

"I have to let you decide."

Hopeless as it seemed, it was in Bert's nature to respond to the idea of the new drug.

"Why not a miracle?" he asked Ann later in Charley's room. Tobey was holding on to the little boy's dry, burning hand, crying under her hair because she did not know what to do. "It's a miracle that I walked again, after they said I'd spend the rest of my life in a wheelchair. Isn't it better to try anything, than just to sit here and watch him die?"

"You could take him home," Ann said. "Hold him. Love him. Surround yourself with friends."

"I'd be afraid," Tobey said, "if he started to bleed a lot at home."

"No, you wouldn't. He would bleed here anyway. You could do what we do." Ann had seen the deaths of too many children in the hospital. She always felt that they should have died at home.

The drug was started. The nurses tried their best with it, but Charley could not tolerate the fierce chemical. It was a relief when the five-day study was ended after two days.

His fine silken hair was quite gone. His old man's scalp was dry and fevered. He was a wasted victim, bruised all over. His lips were raw. The sores crusted around his mouth tore open when he vomited. He was vomiting a lot of blood now.

On the last day of Charley's life, Tobey sat by him and cleaned up the blood. People came in who had known Charley at home, neighbors, his favorite babysitter, parents of children he had played with, the woman from the little grocery store, two young girls who had helped take care of him. Tobey had thought that people would stay away from the death of a child, but they wanted to be there. Someone brought food. Ann saw Tobey, who had thought she would be afraid of the bleeding, eating a sandwich with one hand and cleaning up Charley's blood with the other.

Dr. Truman had thought he was dying at two that morning, but he was still alive at eight, at noon, at six in the evening. Bert talked, to Charley, to himself, to Tobey, to the visitors, to Ann and Joe who came in and out, trying to help the parents to help the child to die. He talked of Charley's whole small life, from the time they took him from the agency through all his discoveries of crawling, standing, tottering, talking, his journeys, his sudden hugs, his relish of himself as so lovable, the old lady on the wharf who rejoiced with him for being without a care.

"Tell him that it's all right to die," Joe wanted to say. He thought that sometimes the dying needed permission from the living before they could let go. He had seen children hang on until the family was there and then die within an hour of the last person arriving.

When Joe's own brother was dying of bone cancer, the whole large family was in the room. He was kept under consciousness with morphine, but he opened his eyes once and asked quite clearly, "What are all you people doing? You all want me to die, don't you?"

Joe was not a nurse then. He was silent, with the rest of his shocked family. Years later, after seeing so many other young people die, he thought that he should have said, because no one else would, "Steve, it's all right. Go ahead and die." He was haunted for a long time by the feeling that he had let his brother down.

Dr. Truman left for home quite late. After spending hours in the hospital, the outside world of Boston where people could walk about and go in and out of restaurants and stand on street corners was a new and beguiling element. Driving out into the fresh, clear night, he saw two young people walking close together by the river. The girl pulled the man's arm to make him stop and look up at the stars. They were smiling, and the phrase came into the doctor's head that Tobey had told him the old lady on Nantucket had used about Charley: "Not a care in the world."

He drove past them and saw that it was Bert and Tobey.

Early in the morning, I went out to the phone by the elevator to call my father in Chicago and tell him that Charley was still alive.

"Everyone's surprised," I said, and he said, "Maybe he'll beat it then, Bert."

"Dad—he's not going to beat it." I hung up. I felt very angry. I thought, How stupid. And then I thought how odd it was that I, who'd always—who'd probably taught my father to say that, and now I was the one to . . .

Just then, Tobey came running down the corridor and told me that Charley had died.

All my life, I've always thought I could beat the odds. Well, as you see, it finally caught up with me. I realize now that life is unfair and arbitrary and things are totally out of control.

We're taught since as long as we can remember to be decent and good. The good guys win—hooray. Well, they don't. They may feel better about themselves, but it's not a ticket to winning. Being good will get you nowhere. You do the best you can, and you get knocked down by something you can't hit back at, and the guy who's never done a decent thing gets away with it. Or doesn't. There's no reason to it. No sense.

I don't ask, "Why Charley? Why us?" It's no use questioning when there's no answer. Things happen. That's all.

People try to explain it: "The will of God." "You've

got a little angel." We don't want an angel. We want our son. "It's part of a master plan," they say. If someone's master plan means making a three-year-old kid suffer more than most people will ever have to—they've got it wrong. They've never thought it through, what kind of God they're talking about who would make a plan like that.

"The Lord only gives you as much sorrow as you can bear," they say. Bullshit! So who'd want to be strong? And I've seen families, at the clinic, at the hospital, crushed by these things. Tobey and I—this drew us totally together, but you see couples disintegrate. Marriages wrecked, jobs lost, they never pick up again, ground into the earth by the loss, by the injustice of it.

Trying to rationalize it makes it worse. It's better to accept that things happen at random. That way you don't kill yourself looking for fairness in a world that isn't fair.

In Charley's room at one time there was a Hindu boy. He had an inoperable brain tumor. His father believed that these kids—his, mine, the other poor little devils on the ward with legs missing, fighting for air with lungs full of tumors—were being punished now for something bad they did in another life. Their suffering would bring them back on a higher level.

I said, "If you really believe that, why is your boy in this hospital? Why not pull out all the tubes, stop the radiation, just let him die?"

He said, "Because it is ordained that you have to live until the last minute."

"Well, that's great." I had to leave the room. His religion had been around for three thousand years, for him to come up with that kind of cruel platitude.

We still feel like parents. We're hoping to get another child. The odds on another adoption are—well. Either we will or we won't. We've started a foundation in Charley's name to be used for leukemia in any way Dr. Truman wants. That's the only way any sense at all can be made out of this, and it doesn't make all that much sense, because it can't help Charley. But to help other kids . . . I try to hang on to that. It's not enough.

If only my son's death could mean that no other child would have to die!

Chapter EIGHT 🌿

$\mathcal{E}$ach couple tries to find reasons for the calamity that attacks their child. There is always the struggle to rationalize, to make some meaning out of it. Even to say, like Bert, "There is no reason" is to state a reason. Randomness. Things happen because they happen.

For Ann and the other parents of leukemia children in the Massachusetts town of Woburn, northwest of Boston, there was a reason: toxic waste.

For more than a hundred years the people of this small industrial town that has housed tanneries and chemical plants have been complaining about pollution. At last, thanks to Ann and many others, something is being done about it.

Ann's son Jimmy got leukemia when he was three. About a year later, a friend told Ann about two other children in the next street who also had it. The friend was trying to say, "You're not the only family to get hit. Other children get leukemia. Look, people survive it. Life goes on."

Ann didn't hear it that way. She had been talking to a local minister who had noticed when he visited the hospital that he saw a surprising number of people from his parish in the clinic where children were getting chemotherapy shots. A year later, there was another child in the same block as Ann, then another, and as time went on and so did Jimmy's sickness, more and more children, until there were twenty-four leukemia cases in Woburn, twelve of them in the half-mile area where Ann lived. Her worry about Jimmy and her frustration and rage at what was happening were crystallized into action.

She and Bruce, the minister, called a meeting of all the leukemia parents, then other meetings for town officials and the whole community.

"You're imagining things," the town moguls blustered, but the press was after them. Innocent children victimized by the criminal carelessness of polluters were hot news. Ann and Bruce were media darlings. Their group was called FACE—For A Cleaner Environment. Town blusterers were forced to take notice, and so eventually were the Commonwealth of Massachusetts and the federal government.

Shy, quiet, self-effacing Ann went down to Washington three times to testify, twice before a congressional committee and once before the Senate. The first time, she was shaking. She died in her shoes. But she did it. And three hundred people listened, and the television crews bathed her in bright light and sent her message out to the whole nation.

Things began to move. Two wells that were found to contain toxic chemicals were closed. A Department of Public Health study revealed that local cancer deaths were among the highest in the state and that the leukemia rate in Ann's small area was seven times greater than normal and twelve times greater for boys.

Although it was not yet officially admitted, a separate study by the Harvard School of Public Health confirmed the link between the wells and the leukemia.

All but two of those children have died. So has Ann's Jimmy. Eight families are suing the two firms who dumped toxic waste directly into the ground or in barrels that leaked into the groundwater aquifer that runs into the wells.

FACE continues to harass officials and industrialists, cut through red tape, and educate a torpid public. They promoted a cancer registry so that a cluster of cancer in one place can be spotted. They were largely responsible for special federal funding to clean up the most dangerous pollution all over the country.

Ann still grieves for Jimmy and misses him terribly and aches for what he had to suffer as he deteriorated and dwindled downward toward a painful death.

"If I was still the old me, I don't think I'd have survived losing him, but the new me has a lot more strength and self-confidence. Friends who used to know me in my old timid days are amazed at what I do. I amaze myself. I'll tackle anyone, talk anywhere, make people listen. I'm fighting to give other children the chance that my poor Jimmy didn't have. In the nine years he was ill, I did everything I could for him. Now this is one last thing I can go on doing."

Parents who aren't caught up in such recognizable toxic tragedies and can't accept the idea of randomness sometimes end up putting the blame on God. But to see the illness of a child as God's *fault* is to make things harder for you. With one hand, you allow yourself dependence on an all-powerful being, and with the other hand, you cheat yourself of that questionable luxury by making him into an incompetent villain.

The people who see it as God's *will* may be better off. They avoid the agonizing anger, but again, there are the self-defeaters who create an image of a deity with total control over their lives and fates and then turn him into a punishing tyrant, with themselves as helpless victims of a God who must be difficult to love.

And there are the self-deluders, who create their God in greeting card style to avoid struggling with unanswerable questions. In another cancer unit in the Bible belt of the Middle West, where there are hymns and laying on of hands as well as chemotherapy, many of the fundamentalist parents take comfort in accepting leukemia and any of its possible outcomes, including death, as God's special purpose.

"God doesn't always want old flowers," they tell each other. "He wants fresh new ones."

*   *   *

Maureen, whose small boy had two years of chemo-therapy after the removal of a tumor, had believed at first that God had dropped this crisis on her and her husband to use them as an example to bring her large fragmented family closer together.

"But that didn't seem fair on poor little William, and what if we failed and it didn't bring the family close? When the idea began not to make sense, I realized it was me, not God, who had invented it, so I washed it out. It was too exhausting anyway. I had enough to do, just concentrating on William.

"Then I felt more at peace. I just prayed for him, and it did help. When they were having a hard time finding a vein, I used to stand there with my eyes shut, holding his hand tight and praying that the needle would go in.

"Not long ago, when we went to the hospital for our quarterly check, I saw a couple whose child was probably going to die. I wanted to tell them what had helped me, but for some stupid reason, I didn't have the nerve. I was afraid they'd laugh at me, or think I was crazy. I was afraid to butt in. I should have, but I didn't.

"You can't intrude your own beliefs." Maureen sighed. "Everyone has to do it their own way."

Rationalizing, reasoning scientifically, accepting unreason, trusting God's purpose—each parent has to find a way that suits them and treat that as the truth. You can't spin around in confusion and dismay. You've got to anchor your belief somewhere.

A psychiatrist who sees many of Dr. Truman's families said, "There's no right way to look at cancer. Whatever is helpful is right, as long as it doesn't interfere with treatment. If someone says, 'It's in God's hands,' I say, 'That's fine, as long as it's in the doctor's hands too.' "

He told me about a family who took a fatally ill boy out in the rain to hear the Pope say Mass on Boston Common. He came back shivering, his thinning hair plastered wetly to his head, teeth chattering. Crazy, said the nurses who were not Irish or Italian or Portuguese or Polish, when he's so vulnerable to viral infection. But the boy did not develop pneumonia. He was a bit better, actually.

Penny, whose two daughters have Ewing's sarcoma, which begins in the marrow spaces of bone shafts, said, "I've always known that God was *there,* but never needed to rely on him. Now I've found out that prayer works. I've seen it happen. I even believe he chose our two girls as special girls. I don't mean that he did this to us, but since it's here, we're to show other people what can be done with it.

"People who've never been through it say that it only happens to those who are strong enough to bear it. That's not true. You get strong, because it's happened. I got strong through faith and prayer, and I don't see how people manage without that. I expect they do have it," she added comfortably, "but they call it something else."

Laura had the same kind of tolerance, in reverse.

"If they want to call it prayer—fine. When Krissie got sick and people said, 'We'll pray for you,' I could interpret that as wishing us well, sending us energy. 'My Yoga group is thinking of you.' Same thing.

"At first when a woman talked about God's will—'God's will, and your cross,' she said—and I yelled, 'No, no, no, no, *no!*' Now if someone says something like, 'God gives us all a cross to bear,' I can see that they're nice people, and I'm nicer now. I've learned to shut up!"

"At Ronald House," where Mary stayed while her teen-age son was in Children's Hospital, "I met this religious woman who thought she'd lost her faith. I didn't think I'd ever had any, but we were both so closely caught up in our children's suffering that we felt the need to stand off a bit and put God in there. So we agreed to pray for each other's children, because that somehow wasn't cheating.

"I'm not talking to God though, after all the relapses, all the things that have gone wrong. I say to *my* God—

the one I'm not talking to—'gimme a break!' "

Joan's son, like Mary's, has Hodgkin's disease. Diagnosed when he was eleven, he had his spleen removed, then radiation and chemotherapy. He was in remission for four years. The treatment was ended. They were within months of being able to call it a cure when he started to complain about back pain.

"He became very sick, but it never occurred to any of us that it might be a relapse. Here I am his mother, a nurse, giving him aspirin for the pain. Here's our local doctor testing his urine and X-raying his kidneys. By the time we took him back to Dr. Truman, he was found to have stage four cancer, a huge mass in the belly, a vertebra and the liver attacked. He was terribly ill, much worse than before. My two other boys were afraid—'Will I get it too?'—even jealous in a guilty sort of way, because Tommy was getting all the favors. The older boy went wild and kicked out a window. I was headed for a breakdown. I'd cry and cry. I thought Tommy would die. I didn't know what to do or who to turn to."

A friend made her go to a Retreat weekend, a sort of short course in Christianity, where people talked about what it had done in their lives.

"I went there fighting and came back in peace. I found—well, that I needn't have a breakdown to escape. There's something else. I know now that there is a living God who's with us whatever we do. Without that, I couldn't have survived. Nor could Tommy.

"He's still in danger, of course. He knows that if the disease comes back, he might die. He's been very angry, rebellious, running away, in trouble at school, aggressive, lashing out at the unfairness of it. Naturally. It *is* unfair. I can accept that though. Life is not fair. That's another freedom I found. Saving energy for things you *can* control."

Sally's form of religion is something like positive thinking.

"That's one reason I like John Truman. He's very positive and hopeful, and he conveys that conviction to you. I have this wonderful Aunt Winnie who totally believes that we are in control of what goes on. 'Katie is doing this to herself,' she tells me, 'and she will cure herself.' I'm not sure yet what that means, but I believe in thinking and talking positively. You don't say, 'If she's cured,' you say, 'When.'

"I took Katie to a faith healer at one point. When I told Dr. Truman, he crossed his arms in Dr. Truman's posture and said what I knew he'd say: 'Fine, as long as she comes in for chemo.' Aunt Winnie said, 'Faith without acts is nothing. Doctors and healers are here to help us, but we must help ourselves.' I like that.

"Katie's chance of a cure is given as seventy percent over seven years. Well, forget thirty. I know—I just *know* that she's going to be in that seventy."

Small Katie, who has been playing with a car on the floor and hasn't seemed to be listening, comes to my knee, huge round eyes in a composed Victorian face with a mouth like a folded flower, and whispers, *"I know."*

Then she goes back to the floor and pushes the car to a tuneless song. "I know . . . I know . . . I know."

For these smaller children who are too young to understand what is going on, or to be scarred by frightening or painful memories, it is also very unfair, but they don't know it. That burden falls on the parents, along with the endless and exhausting job of seeing the child through the drastic treatment and its possible variety of distressing side effects.

Deborah took David through three years of chemotherapy, lumbar punctures, bone marrow tests, and the cranial radiation that the hospital was using at that time to knock out leukemia cells in the central nervous system.

At first, they made the journey to the hospital almost every day. Then once a week, then once a month, then every two months. After two years of remission, David was leading a fairly normal life without much sickness, and after three years, they took him off all the pills.

This is the day you long for and dream about. The family makes a ceremony of flushing all the rest of the hated pills down the drain. It is supposed to be a time of celebration, and you are ashamed to find yourself suddenly sad and abandoned and afraid.

You feel you have lost the shelter of the doctors and nurses and the hospital. You have lost your job with the pills and the clinic visits. *Will Dr. Truman and Monica and Sue remember us?* There is nothing more you have to do, and the tired tears that come easily now are half relief, half anticlimax.

"Isn't it wonderful that he's cured!" people exclaim, and you say yes and burst into tears.

You have got used to the idea that chemotherapy must go on for a long time in case there are cancer cells lurking. *Why have they stopped it now? How do they know there's not one cell left?*

When Deborah brought David back for his three-months check, then at six months, then once a year, she would be tense with the same old fear. *Will this be the time they find something wrong?*

Everyone was so pleased and optimistic, but she never got over the fear of a relapse. They teased her at the clinic. "Relax, you're making us nervous." But she could never calm down until she knew the test results.

Perhaps she was looking ahead defensively, to prepare herself, just in case. Perhaps she was being pulled defensively back to all the years of anxiety and pain.

Where had all those years of her twenties gone? David could not remember them, but Deborah would never forget. If she could find a reason for what had happened to her, she might be able to let go of it.

Why him? Why us? Why me? Some day she might understand the reason. Not now.

*   *   *

"What's it all *for?*" Clara agonizes. "Why us? Why her? She's so little."

Maria is four now, and her two years of treatment have gone well, but her young mother is sometimes overwhelmed with despair at the unfairness of her life. Her childhood was strict and unhappy, with a gloomy, anxiety-ridden father who hardly let her cross the street alone, and her growing up was overloaded with the burdens of a large, helpless family who picked her as their pack mule.

She married Dick too young, for escape as well as for love, and before they had time to build their life, she was knocked out by rheumatoid arthritis. Pain, lameness, drugs, a bone operation right after Maria's birth, increasing difficulty in caring for the baby, and then the final blow, delivered by Dr. Truman coming into an outpatient room at four o'clock.

"I remember the time exactly, and the jolt of the electric clock hand, and the look on his face. That look I will hold with me forever. He shut the door and said, 'Leukemia.'

"I didn't believe him. 'Couldn't it be wrong?' I kept asking, and my husband was weeping, and my daughter was on the bed vomiting and crying, 'Daddy, what's the matter?'

"It was so unfair on her. Unfair on all of us. Dick had been through all that with my operation, having to take care of me and the baby. Now this, for him. My family still expected me to be the one who was strong, to listen to their woes and difficulties and whining about nothing.

"Calling me up when they heard about Maria to go, 'Oh oh, doom and gloom, I can't bear it,' and I'd think, *You can't bear it? Are you crazy? This is my problem.*

"And I was still supposed to hold up the wall for them. I'm always there for them and nobody's there for me.

"When Maria came down with leukemia, I thought then, I can remember, I thought, *I . . . will . . . never . . . be . . . happy . . . again.* Even if the treatment gets rid of it, there'll always be that fear that it could come back. I'd have to go through it all again and be the strong one, and I couldn't do it. I wouldn't do it."

"You would though," I said.

Clara thought about that and sighed. "All right, I would. I couldn't, but I would. What else is there ever to do?"

She cried openly with her face up, looking at me, the heavy black hair behind her shoulders tilting back her head.

"Dick and I—we never got a break. All my entire life, why don't I get a break? Why don't I ever get a stinking break?"

Why us? Why always us?

Carol's father lost his job the week after his older daughter had to have her leg amputated. That was his breaking point. Being fired was a humiliating personal injury that made him ask miserably, "What's wrong with us? What have we done so bad in our lives that this has to happen to us?"

Her mother crumpled after two years of being strong through bone cancer attacking first her younger daughter, and then her older daughter more severely.

When Carol was able to move about the house and take care of herself, Penny and her husband could at last go away for a holiday. Not a proper holiday. Just a weekend. Not even a proper weekend. Just one night in a motel. They came home to a burst pipe and the house flooded. Penny waded in and poked holes in the ceiling, put buckets under them, wrung out mops, put towels down, swept water out of the back door, did all the right things. Until she went into the dining room that was fairly dry and saw that the kittens had pulled over and destroyed her great cascading fern that had thrived on the last two years of neglect that had disabled the other plants.

She went to pieces. She sat on the damp carpet and

sobbed. "Why, why, why? Why does everything go wrong?"

Her husband said, "Hey, come on, after what you've been through. Falling apart over a plant, for God's sake. I'll get you another."

"I don't want another. I wanted that one." But it wasn't the plant. It was everything, and the plant had just pushed her over the edge.

"This has changed my ideas about life."

Jane's son is very young, a sturdy, bright-skinned boy of three with fat cheeks from prednisone and thin yellow hair. When Sue skillfully slips the needle into his vein at the clinic, he shrieks like a pig-killing, "Mummy! Mummy!" sobbing and trembling all the time the syringe slowly pushes the drug in, while Jane can only hold him, but cannot be the rescuing mother who makes it all better.

"When he got so sick and we knew what it was, it made me feel very bad about life. It made me feel, what's the point? Life is too painful. Everyone dies. Anyone might get cancer. I'm young and I used to love life, but there was a time during this illness when I almost didn't want my son to live, if it's such a horrible world to grow up in.

"He's too little to know he's ill, so we bear the weight of the illness." Weeping, Jane said, "We are the ones with the cancer really. The parents are the victims."

It is painful to put these things down on the page. It was with pain that I listened to them, with pain that they were told, but they are things that needed to be said. It is not self-pity to share pain. Self-pity is when you brood over it and nurse it to yourself and fondle it: "Poor me." Comforting at first, in a sneaky illicit way, like a drink at the wrong time of day, but it can turn on you, like secret drinking, and become a crippling habit.

To cry "Poor me" to someone once in a while is a harmless indulgence. You don't want anything done about it.

You know it can't be taken away. You just want someone to know about it.

The mothers who did cry are all strong and steadfast. None of them has gone under, or let their sick child down, or anyone else. They are extremely honest. Crisis has scoured their lives clean of pretense. That's why they can let go occasionally and then go back to being strong.

Chapter N I N E 🌿

The children are so strong. Oh my God, are they patient and brave and unbelievably enduring.

They suffer, but they try to spare their family suffering. They don't use their illness as an excuse to get attention, or to hold their parents in thrall, or to behave any old way they want. They learn to accept the disease as part of themselves, in an amazingly mature way that many grown-ups can't achieve. They understand its symptoms and its treatment and tell Sue and Monica what treatment they've come in for before their charts are opened.

They take charge of their own chemotherapy at home, keeping charts and laying out seventeen pills on the kitchen counter and deciding when the drugs aren't going to stay down anymore and it is time to have them intravenously.

"It was terrible at first," Chris remembers. "Pills weren't in my schedule for the day. I've always had this great system. My sister, she'll get up two hours before the school bus and try out her whole wardrobe. Me, I'd get up ten minutes before the bus, dress, eat breakfast, and get out and down to the corner just as the bus brakes. The pills were so hard to swallow, one by one. It took too long. So I had to get a system for that. If you don't swallow them, they dissolve and taste awful. So I taught myself to take the whole dose—twenty-five pills at once, gulp—in one small glass of water. Now I get up eleven minutes before the bus. That's all."

If children come from a shredded family where nobody

wants the bother of bringing them in, they get themselves to the hospital for treatment. Sometimes the parents do want to bring them in, but the child—even a child of eleven or twelve—insists on coming alone, to spare the family, and because it helps to be independent.

They leave the hospital with a brain tumor to take college entrance exams, although they don't expect to be alive by the start of the university year. They usually know they are dying before anyone tells them, but they don't talk about it until the doctor has told their parents.

A lot of the little ones don't cry anymore at the needles for drugs, bone marrow samples, or lumbar punctures. They sit very quietly in the front seat of the car and ask, as they are turning in to the hospital parking lot, "Is it my hand today, or my back?"

When the bigger ones get tense and jittery the night before chemotherapy, the hospital staff calls the syndrome "Chemokid." They have so few veins left that will take a needle. They have learned that they need not let medical students poke for a vein, and how many tries an intern can have. But even with the finest needle and the gentlest skills, the Chemokids are anxious and afraid. They don't say much.

"What do you want for Christmas?" Laura asked Krissie.

"New veins."

Sometimes they fall apart when they learn that they will lose all their hair, but receive stoically the news of amputation.

"If my leg is going to kill me, I don't want it," Krissie insisted on the risky ordeal of having her leg amputated and her lung tumors removed at the same time.

"You get me once," she told the surgeon. "I'm not going down there again and again and let you cut me up piecemeal—my leg, then one lung, then the other lung. I'd rather die now than go bit by bit."

After five hours, she came up again in the elevator, a

skinny, bald, one-legged teenager, wrapped up like a corpse, but she was talking.

"I fooled them, didn't I? I came back."

Carol went to surgery with a red ribbon on the toe of the leg she was going to lose to save her life, and a label: HANDLE WITH CARE.

She came home in less than a week, because it was Christmas. Her father wanted to carry her up to bed, but she crawled up the stairs by herself.

Like their parents, the strong children sometimes break down over unfairness. The last straw for both Carol and Krissie was having to suffer the agonizing "phantom pains" from the injured nerve endings of the leg that wasn't there.

"It's not fair that they don't tell you beforehand," Carol said. "But even if they did, you wouldn't believe it. You would never believe that the foot would come back and hurt so much that you'd want to tear it off again."

Krissie, who was able to convert bitterness into rational fantasies, decided, "I've behaved better than anyone else, so I've been rewarded with worse pains than anyone else. So because that's not fair, it allows me to let go and scream."

The basic unfairness of "Why me?" is so vast and obvious that it is not often voiced by the children. It sometimes surfaces in serious speculation, not conceited but honest, about why the good guys get nailed and the jerks go free.

Carol: "I'm an athlete. I'm a dancer. I've trained that leg to do strong and graceful things. I've kept myself healthy, eaten right, stayed away from drugs and alcohol. There's these kids that abuse their bodies like crazy, and nothing ever happens to them."

Brian: "Everything was going so great. I was into a lot of good stuff, not just for myself, but—well, I thought I was helping people. You know how it is. When you're little, you could get sick and die and it wouldn't make any difference to the world, except to your family. Then you begin to matter to people, you count a bit in their lives. Maybe they need you. You see these drop-outs that are never going to be any use to anybody. Why don't they get sick?"

Joe: "I think people like me. There's a lot of people I love. What did I do to get picked for Hodgkin's? In this family—Grandma, the uncles, everybody—aren't I sort of—you know, like the favorite child?"

It is the favorite children who get chosen, the mothers think. The special ones. The best.

They see the sick children as rare and heroic, and they all talked to me about the strength these children have. If the parents have done well, they insist, it is because their child has shown them how.

"Martha was always extraordinary, even as a very little girl. People noticed her. People were drawn to her. She seemed somehow—extra alive, as if she were preparing herself for what she had to face."

"From the time Jimmy was born, he was my special child. He was like an appendage. I couldn't go anywhere without him. Couldn't even turn my back. If I went out in the evening, I had to wait till he was in bed and then put a robe and slippers on over my dress to kiss him goodnight, so he wouldn't know.

"He always wanted me with him. And you respond to that. He was special to me and he made me feel really special, because I was so important to him."

"Paul lived a year and a half after that hotshot doctor said, 'You're terminal now, Paul.' He was incredible. He was so positive. So up. He had a lot of positive energy, and that kept me going. After he died, it was more than the devastating loss. Without him, my life came apart and there was no one to help me pull it back together."

"Brian was a very soft and gentle kind of child, but dogged. He'd try and try with some toy that was too old for him, determined to make it work. He never gave up on his sports, even when he was too dizzy to see the ball, and he was like that with his treatment. A hero. I couldn't lose hope, because he didn't. Right to the end."

Deborah had always seen David as a shining child.

"Somehow—and I've seen this in other children at the hospital—godlike. Very generous and kind. We always said he'd be easy to kidnap. He was so loving and open and he trusted everyone. He still does, even after all he's been through."

Deborah used to think that David was the favorite patient in the hospital. He never had tantrums in the parking garage, whose echoes magnify the distress of children who don't want to get out of the car. He never cried in the waiting room, and although his friends in the clinic had to hurt him and stick needles in him, he hustled in ahead of his mother with a shining smile, sure of the welcome he always got.

No doubt other mothers were convinced that their brave, angelic child was everybody's favorite, but there did seem to be something about David. People were drawn to him. They seemed compelled to give him things—toys, a picture, a ball, a coin—and often he would give them away in a careful, benevolent way to another child. One of the nurses' aides gave him a battered old teddy bear with one ear, no eyes, and a chewed red ribbon. It had belonged to her son who had died five years ago. She had thought she would keep the bear always, but she gave it to David.

Once he reduced Dr. Truman to tears. He had to have a spinal tap, a gruesome procedure at any age, extra frightening for a small child not to be able to see what is going on behind his back.

It was explained to him that because he was sick, Dr. Truman wanted to do something to make him better. "Because he loves you, David," Deborah said. "If it hurts, remember that it's because he loves you."

The spinal was horrendous, difficult, and painful. It took Cindy and Monica and another nurse to hold him still, while he yelled and sobbed and struggled. When it was almost over, the tiny little boy, soaked all over in sweat and tears, got his bald head free to turn it and look up at the tall doctor above him, and through his sobbing, managed to gasp, "Thank you, Dr. Tooman, for my hurting."

How could anyone stand that? The doctor grimaced, his eyes full of tears. Cindy and the nurses were in no better shape. Deborah and Dave, who were always both there for spinals, were undone.

"My God," Dave said afterward, "have we laid it on too thick about the lovely hospital where everybody loves him? Poor little kid, we never asked him for this."

But that was the kind of child he was, and for all he knew, at three-and-a-half years old, everybody had to go through this.

Chapter **T E N** 🌿

"**A**t that time," Mary Lou said, "when Nicole had lost her sight and they were having such a hard time getting into her veins, she was amazingly calm and good about it. We had been through so much already. I was going crazy because the interns who were trying to set up the intravenous were messing her about. But Nicole just lay there, one eye closed and one eye open but not seeing, and asked me patiently, 'Are they almost done, Mummy?'"

Nicole was the sickest surviving patient John Truman has ever had in his seventeen years of practice. How sick can you get and still survive? Nicole is one answer.

Nicole was admitted to the hospital when she was two and a half with acute myelocytic leukemia, which is more serious than the lymphocytic type, and usually, like the chronic phase that Jill came in with, only seen in adults.

Her mother lived close to the hospital and so went home to sleep. One night she woke suddenly from a terrifying dream of her child standing silently by her bed with blood dripping from her nose.

It was so vivid that when Mary Lou opened her eyes, she expected to see Nicole actually there with blood all over her face.

She woke her husband and they dressed and went to the hospital. The leukemia had caused several hemorrhages in the child's brain. They found her dazed, one eye closed, one side paralyzed, hardly able to speak.

Normally, if you can call any kind of cancer normal, it

takes from two to three weeks to gain remission. It was much longer for Nicole. One eye was all right. The other had no sight.

One morning when Mary Lou went early to the hospital, Nicole woke but did not look at her mother or say anything. When Mary Lou handed her a box of little cars she liked, she reached in and chose one by feel, without looking.

Her father came in on his way to work.

"I don't think she can see at all," Mary Lou whispered.

To test Nicole, he held up some of her stuffed animals, and she told him who was who. When the doctor came to examine her, he told them the sight of both eyes was gone now. The three-year-old child had been guessing the animals so they would not know.

Nicole was in the hospital for months. Mary Lou's whole lonely, anxious life was there. She did not want visitors, because they took time away from her daughter who might be dying, and she did not want anyone to see how sick Nicole was and how awful she looked.

One day Mary Lou was dozing by the bed where the child lay in a deep flat sleep as if she had been thrown down on the mattress, with one arm flung out for the tubing and the drugs, which seemed to be less and less effective. Her marrow counts improved sometimes, and Mary Lou would know that she was right to go on hoping. The next day, the counts would be dangerously low again.

As she sat by the bed, half awake and half asleep, a voice that was not a dream said gently but quite firmly, *"My child."*

It was then that Dr. Truman came in with a very sad face and said, "I'm afraid I have to tell you that we don't see any hope for Nicole. I'm so sorry." He looked away from Mary Lou to the sleeping child. "I don't think I've ever had to give parents so much bad news."

When he looked back at Mary Lou, she was smiling.

"Don't be sorry," she said, "because I think you're wrong. I think we're at the end of the line. This is going to be the turnaround."

"I hope you're right." Doubt had replaced his usual optimism.

"I know I am."

He looked closely at her. "Yes," he said. "Yes, you do."

The doctors had decided to try some of the old outdated drugs of five or six years ago, as a last resort. Nicole should go home, since she might not have more than a month to live.

The day they took her home, she ate a large Easter meal of ham and sweet potatoes and did not lose it half an hour later. The change of drugs did not make her sick. After a few days, to the surprise of everyone except Mary Lou, Nicole was finally in remission.

She was blind, free of cancer, but desperately vulnerable to any infection. Pneumonia was the next bad news that Dr. Truman had to give. Nicole was back in the hospital for months, a lot of the time on a respirator, because she could hardly breathe. One doctor said he thought her lungs were gone, and although the leukemia was checked, this would be what would kill her.

Nicole had had so many intravenous transfusions that it became harder and harder to get a needle into her collapsed veins. She was endlessly patient, even when one of the interns, after an hour of trying unsuccessfully for a vein in several different places, had to cut down once more with a scalpel into a leg vein.

"Are they nearly finished?"

The intern's not-very-skillful cut down was finished, but the next bad news was only just beginning.

The next day, Nicole's leg was swollen and very painful. There was an infection from the vein into the knee, which developed into osteomyelitis.

They had to operate, even though her lungs were not fit for an anesthetic. She had about eight operations on that badly infected knee and was in the hospital another six months.

Battered, exhausted, aching all the time for what her child had to go through, Mary Lou still never lost the spark of hope that had been kindled in her when the voice spoke through her waking doze. She guarded Nicole like a tigress, always questioning, making sure she knew what was being done, talking to the nurses and doctors, watching the intravenous drips, doing most of the nursing herself, opposing a resident who wanted to take out the lung tubes when Mary Lou knew the specialist had decided to leave them in, fighting off an intern who came in to cut down into a vein in the other leg.

"Not again."

"We have to. She has no more veins I can get a needle into."

"Get someone else. We'll find a vein."

Before the last operation to scrape infection from the bone, the surgeon said, "This is it, you know. After this, we shall have to amputate."

Well then, thought Mary Lou, astonished at herself for once more knowing more than the doctors, *this is it. It always has to go to the eleventh hour, to the brink of total disaster, and then it turns around and starts to go the other way.*

Anyone trying to find reasons why some people go through life more or less unscathed and others are attacked by one cudgel blow after another, would have a difficult time with Nicole's early life. Soon after she went home, with a badly gouged and scarred knee that would need plastic surgery later, her temperature shot up to delirium. She vomited constantly. She had meningitis.

In the hospital, seizures took away her speech again. She moved her mouth and tried to make words, and when she couldn't, she started to invent signs for what she wanted.

On the way home again at last, sitting in the front of the car, she put out a hand and patted her father on the knee while he was driving, and said, "Daddy."

Her speech came back gradually, to leave her now with only occasional hesitations over a word. Her parents suggest, "Choose another word," which often helps with stammerers, but she won't. As with everything else, she has to work at the original word stubbornly, until she can say it.

One night when she had felt her way to bed, moving about her room with the assurance she had learned during her blindness, her mother sat on the bed and finished reading a story, then kissed her goodnight and went out, turning off the light.

Nicole called out, "Please leave the light on!"

Light perception had come back. Then color came. Then a small amount of vision in the bottom quarter of one eye.

Now at thirteen, she is able to read one letter at a time in large print books, or by way of a video camera that converts print into letters on a television screen. She has one of these machines at home and one at school, both given to her by the Lions, who understand practical generosity.

She is bright and quick at school. When her dancing class puts on a show, she does a solo tap, although she can't see where she is on stage. Both eyes are wide open and though they don't follow you, they look so normal and she manages so well that she fools even doctors at the hospital, who are apt to tell Mary Lou, "Her sight is getting better."

It isn't, but her life is, all the time. She has weathered two further operations. One was to adjust some internal difficulties, and another to make her good leg the same length as her damaged one, which had missed some growth. She does almost everything the other children do, and although she has missed so much school, she now keeps up with the rest of the class. She can write and work with figures, using her camera and screen, and is beginning some special training in computers.

She has been off chemotherapy for three years and in another year can be called cured. She was the sickest patient Dr. Truman ever had and is one of his longest-surviving patients with acute myelocytic leukemia.

A miracle? Mary Lou seriously considers that.

"I knew it could happen. No. I really didn't know. But I never stopped hoping."

While we are talking, Nicole runs in from the garden at the back of the apartments and slams the door. She is angry. Some boys have been hiding from her and calling her blind.

"Tell them I can see."

While Mary Lou goes down to find the boys, Nicole takes me into her bedroom to read to me. She clears a clutter of books and clothes from a table to the floor and lays a book open under the video camera that transfers each line into huge letters on the bright screen of a large television set.

Small for her age, resolute, standing with her right eye so close that the dark lashes brush the screen, she reads the words to me, one letter at a time.

Another of the sickest patients was Judy's son Christopher, who is now fifteen, but almost didn't get beyond eight. When he's mentioned in the clinic, Dr. Truman adds, "Damn near died."

After three years in remission, he relapsed with a further invasion of cancer cells. A strep infection got into his blood through a biopsy area, and both his legs became gangrenous. Long scars are on his legs now where the bones had to be cleaned out and the surgery wounds left open for irrigation and draining.

Judy had always had a fearful premonition that this third child of her four would not grow up. She began to accept the fact that he would die now, but the spirit in the child did not. With morphine to help him through the Chinese torture of the irrigation, he taught his mother that she was wrong. She could forget her premonition. He was not going to be Christopher who died, but Christopher who damn near died.

*   *   *

In a summer town on the shore south of Boston, I am having breakfast with Marion at the high counter that divides her kitchen and living room.

I look out behind her at a thicket of rocking masts in the estuary of the wide marshy river. She looks over my shoulder at the stormy Atlantic, pounding in across three thousand miles from Spain to foam against the sea wall below her house.

She, like Mary Lou, is also considering the possibility of a miracle. Her daughter Carla is another of the sickest survivors, a living example of how much punishment the human body can take and still restore itself.

"Carla was thirteen and the growth was behind her knee. That's an unusual place for Ewing's sarcoma, which was the best thing it could be if it had to be cancer. The radiologist was certain it was osteogenic sarcoma. That's the kind of bone cancer that could mean she'd have to lose her leg.

"We weren't going to tell her what they thought, but the night before the biopsy, when she was watching television in the hospital, the surgeon's assistant came in and started talking—I could have shot him—about how they make great artificial limbs these days, and girls wear pants anyhow, so no one sees. She went on watching some dumb program on television without paying attention.

"We were new in the hospital, so I said, 'Carla, do you hear Dr.—?' I've forgotten his name, I don't care to remember him—'Do you hear him talking to you?'

" 'I hear him,' she said, her eyes still on the television hanging from the ceiling, 'but it's not going to be like that. I'm not going to lose my leg.'

" 'She's not going to lose her leg,' I told Dr. Whatsit, and he went out.

"I'd been terrified of that from the beginning." Under her short curly hair, Marion's eyes are very blue and her face is very brown from living on the edge of the ocean. "Her life was in danger, but I was obsessed only by the idea that I wasn't going to let her lose her leg.

"Before the biopsy, which the surgeon thought would confirm that it was osteogenic, they sent her home for Christmas."

The stories of parents are peppered with memories of Christmases, tense, bereft, or rejoicing. Christmas a stable landmark in a calendar gone crazy. Christmas is one of the few things you still do, of all the other things you don't do.

"I never want to go through a Christmas like 1975. All my girls were happy. Even Carla. She didn't know then that she had cancer. We were none of us sure, but after the biopsy, then we'd have to know the worst. And I thought—here in this kitchen, it was, I'm always in the kitchen, feeding people—if it's such a lost cause, I'd better try Saint Jude.

"After the biopsy, the surgeon called us. He said, 'It's cancer, but we're not going to have to amputate her leg, because it's not that form of sarcoma.'

"The radiologist, a top man at the hospital, couldn't believe it. He said, 'I'd have staked my career it was osteogenic,' and I thought, *Hm. You'd stake your career, but I staked Saint Jude.*"

The wind was getting up. Behind me, one of the big windows over the sea wall rattled impatiently and the house shuddered. In the great nor'easter of 1978, this house's predecessor was washed away in a bundle of sticks and shingles. In front of me, the masts danced in the harbor with the rapid ting-ting-ting of halyards against metal.

" 'We can save her leg,' the surgeon said. 'Now it's a matter of saving her life.'

"It was easier now. My obsession about her leg was simplified to: I'm not going to let her die.

"By science now, not by miracles. Carla had radiation and two years of chemotherapy, and she was so very sick that there must have been times when she would rather have been dead, but she never said so. She doesn't talk much. She keeps things inside.

"For some reason, the chemo affected her worse than any other patient they'd ever had there. They had to give all the drugs intravenously, otherwise she'd vomit them right back. Sometimes she'd lose seven or eight pounds in a week. Dr. Truman tried marijuana to control the nausea, and hypnosis, in case it was psychosomatic. The days she had to have Cytoxan, she'd cry silently on the drive in and start to feel sick before we ever got there.

"I remember the first time she met Jen, the nurse-practitioner who was there before Sue. She'd been sick all night, and when Jen came into the waiting room with her hands held out to welcome her, Carla threw up into them.

" 'Well,' Jen said. 'Don't get personal.'

"Some of the drugs like Cytoxan were so powerful that she'd go on throwing up in the car and at home, every fifteen minutes, right through till five in the morning. I'd be with her all night with towels and basins. We'd doze a few minutes, and then she'd wake again and be wrenched apart. Sometimes before I went back to the other bed, she'd catch my hand and say, 'I'm sorry to keep you awake.' That was the only time I was afraid I'd cry. I had to turn my head away."

It was at that point that Marion and I both cried, looking at each other helplessly across the kitchen counter.

"Constantly . . . for two years . . . she constantly apologized to me and thanked me for helping her."

These are not saints. They are ordinary children, and they pick up their ordinary lives whenever they can. Between treatments Carla went back to baby-sitting, and although her leg muscles were damaged from the radiation, she would limp off down the sandy road behind the house to her job at the local fruit and vegetable stand.

In the third year of treatment, Carla at fifteen insisted on going to the hospital alone. She marched into the clinic and refused to take the Cytoxan.

"You're supposed to take it for two more months."

"If two years hasn't done it, two months won't make

any difference. It's my body and I refuse it, because it's too hard on my mother at home. That's it."

Dr. Truman and Monica and Jen listened seriously and agreed. "She may be right. We've done enough damage."

"I was petrified," Marion remembers. "I imagined she'd die the next day. But she went on with the other drugs that didn't affect her so horribly."

"Did she ever imagine herself dying?"

"Once after a boy she loved in the hospital had died, she asked me, 'Am I going to die?'

"I said no. I wasn't going to let her.

" 'Okay,' she said, 'I just wanted to know.'

"She was so strong. Her courage and determination helped me to be strong. We did it together. She's been off chemo four years now, but I'm afraid to say 'cured' in case something happens.

"I don't plan ahead anymore. That's what it does to you.

"I used to worry about everything and everyone, and what would happen. In those good old days when nothing happened, I used to wonder: Why not? Why not me? I'm no different from anybody else. Why do we get benefits we don't deserve?

"And now that we've seen other children die, some we were very close to, three of them with Carla's type of tumor, because it spread to the lungs, I still wonder: Why not us? What does it mean, that Carla's alive? What's the reason she got sick and now she's well? Is there something she and I are supposed to do?"

Chapter ELEVEN 🌿

*P*erhaps one reason why parents continue to grope for a meaning, a reason for the illness, is to try to ward off the demon of their own irrational guilt, the most destructive of all the self-defeating human emotions.

Why should these parents blame themselves? They shouldn't, but useless guilt is a lurking enemy for all of us, and the illness of a child is a fertile field where guilt sneaks in however hard you try, like weeds where you think you have sown only vegetables.

Helen's family does not run to doctors for every least little thing. "We try to cure ourselves. So there was I, feeding chicken soup to Polly and getting her out in the sun because she was so pale, and all the time the cancer cells were dividing and dividing in her blood."

"If you had brought her in earlier," Monica reminds her, "it might have been too soon to diagnose leukemia."

"You say that to make me feel better. But guilt is guilt. If you feel it, you feel it, and no one can make it go away."

When there are no reasons for guilt, these damned mothers invent them as part of the pain. Jerri's daughter Karyn had been born with an extra toe. When she got leukemia, Jerri thought, *Can't I do anything right? My God, I couldn't even have a baby with the right number of toes, and now look what I've done.*

A sample of the illogical litany with which some of these noble fools conjure up guilt, in order to avoid feeling guilty about not feeling guilty:

I was too old/young to have a baby.

I should have breast-fed her.

I started her on solid food too late.

I smoked/drank/rode a horse/was depressed during my pregnancy.

It was the ant powder I put down.

We shouldn't have dug the well. There's something in the water.

Now they're saying that cancer *is* hereditary.

We shouldn't have had a child.

We shouldn't have gone to Bermuda without her.

Why didn't I insist on blood tests?

Two blondes shouldn't marry. Look at all those yellow-haired children in the clinic.

Why did I give him cow's milk?

If I hadn't left my husband . . .

If I'd had the guts to leave my husband when he was drinking . . .

Why didn't the boarding school call me? What's wrong with *me* that they didn't call me till the tumors were as big as oranges?

I should have known that babies don't cry like that for nothing.

When she whined to be picked up, I accused her— accused her, at two years old—of being jealous of the new baby.

My daughter Pam, who did all the right things for her sick baby and nursed him day and night in the hospital, felt guilty because she could not cut herself in two and also be with the other twin.

The rest of the family, the brothers and sisters of the sick child—another easy focus for irrational guilt. But how can you do it all? At the beginning, the one who has cancer needs all your time and energy. That is the great challenge. You are in the battle lines of the fight against the invader. How can you take care of the troops in the rear? One of the hardest things about the whole grueling business is balancing your life between the child in crisis and the others who need you too.

Arrangements are made for someone to take care of them: grandparents, aunts, friends, neighbors. The younger ones can probably adjust all right as long as they feel safe. When Ann was with Jimmy on the ward, she would dash briefly back to her mother's house whenever she could, not only to see that the other children were all right, but so that her mother could see that *she* was all right.

The older children who understand more of what is going on will suffer more than the younger ones. What does the illness do to these brothers and sisters?

Even though their parents try to stretch themselves in all directions, they are bound to feel the loss of attention. "I turned against my mother because she had to turn away from me," one sister told me. Another became very depressed as she went into her teens. She had been a dissatisfied and moody girl before. The death of her older sister proved to her that life is a cheat and a disaster. She has made one suicide attempt and is having a very hard time struggling out of depression.

A brother resented his sick brother for being in the limelight.

"People fell over themselves giving him all kinds of presents, wanting to take him to Disney World. He didn't even want the toys and games and stuff. He used to share them with me, but I didn't want them, because they hadn't been given to *me*. I was jealous of him. I'll admit that.

Crazy, when he was so sick. But there were times when I wanted to be sick, too. I used to cough and have aches and pains. I guess you could call me a hypochondriac. I still catch myself making too much of a cold or a headache. Like, 'Gimme a Band-Aid!' "

"It was unfair," another honest brother said. "Things had been going well for us. This was the first bad thing in our family, and it didn't only happen to my sister. It happened to all of us."

A sister talked about anxiety. "She was only twelve. I was older, but I couldn't have been so brave about it if it was me. I knew she might die. I was scared for her, but I was scared for myself too. Cancer is frightening. It's in the family now, I thought. I started to think pimples were skin cancer. I'd come home and complain, 'I've got a pain in my leg.' My mother would look at me and she'd know what I was thinking, and she'd answer, 'No, you don't have cancer.' "

The brother of a boy who died said, "He had more to offer than any of us. Why did it happen to him and not to me? I thought it was my fault. When we used to fight, before he got sick, I'd sometimes tell him, 'Drop dead!' You know, like you do to a brother. I couldn't tell anyone about that, because things were so awful, I couldn't risk them hating me. Finally I was able to tell one of my older cousins. He was good. He didn't say, 'Oh, that's ridiculous.' He let me say it. He agreed it was a rotten way for me to feel. Then he explained more about the disease and why it had nothing to do with me."

When Jimmy was too ill to lead a normal child's life, his mother wanted to beg his brother, "Please don't go!" if Chuckie was invited somewhere where Jimmy couldn't go. But she couldn't hold him back. She knew he had to go, although he was torn, as she was, between his need for independence and wanting to protect Jimmy.

Even when Jimmy was well enough to go out and play with the other boys his age, it was difficult for him. He was too weak and small. They had grown and he hadn't, because of the chemotherapy, and he'd been out of things for so long that he didn't know the games they were playing now. Chuckie, who was a bit older and much bigger, was very helpful and protective. He always made sure that Jimmy was included in what the others were doing. If they teased Jimmy for being bald and thin and stumbly, Chuckie would show them a fist and growl, "You better not say anything about my brother when I'm around."

Krissie's sister Lesley told me, "We were always a close family, and when she got sarcoma, it sort of brought us closer, all four of us. It became a way of life. You get used to it. My parents encouraged me to lead my own life and get into all sorts of sports and things. Being younger, I stayed with my grandparents quite a bit. I liked that. I was special to them. My grandfather runs a school for handicapped children, so I went to school there. I was less upset when Krissie had to lose her leg, because I knew people at school with worse handicaps. 'Big deal,' I said to Krissie. 'I have a friend who doesn't have any legs at all.'

"Krissie and I were very close. When she died, I thought none of us would ever be happy again. But we are."

She ran a finger under her eyelids and manufactured a smile. Krissie was very brave, greathearted, and Lesley is made of the same stuff. "It's all *right*," she said through tears that fell into the corners of the smile. "I promise you. It's all right. It's just that I feel so bad for her. She missed what I'm having. Life. A future. Not so much having the future when it comes, but the thought of it now. Krissie was funny. She could always make me laugh. I miss that. But it's all *right*. Truly it is."

What does the serious illness of a child do to a marriage? It depends on the two people involved, and the kind of marriage it was to start with.

Dr. Truman observes, with his clinician's penchant for

139

percentages, "A hundred percent of the mothers cope nobly and well. Of the men, I have to say that only about thirty-three percent do that. Those men will share the tasks, support the wife's strengths, prop her up when she flags, spend as much time at the hospital as they can, be absolutely marvelous in every way, and tremendous help to the doctor, and the child's recovery.

"The middle thirty-three percent do an adequate job. They don't disgrace themselves, but they don't go overboard either. We don't see much of them in the clinic or on the ward, and it's usually the wife who talks to the doctor and gets the information and makes the decisions.

"The bottom thirty-three percent simply bow out and leave the wife to do it all by herself.

"Women always rise to the occasion." He thought a bit and smiled. He likes to think about the mothers. "Men may or may not rise. When they rise, they rise with splendor. When they don't rise, they can be positive cads." Because he is a literary doctor, his conversation is colored here and there with Victoriana. "There are chilling stories of fathers who, because they couldn't deal with the child's cancer, have said in effect, 'I wash my hands of this. It's your business. Sink or swim by yourself.' And disappeared."

Not every man who fails to rise in splendor goes that far in caddishness. He stays around, but he dumps the whole responsibility onto his wife and expects her to manage the sick child, the other children who aren't sick, and sometimes himself who is sick with the self-centeredness of insecurity.

Harry was five years older than Alice, but he was dependent on her and demanding of her, not unlike his four-year-old son Jeff. Alice went along with it. She loved him. She was very young. She did not know what else to do.

Until Jeff got leukemia and she had to give him all her time. Harry would not stay the night with her on the ward, and he hated being in the house without her and having to do un-Harry types of things like water plants and do his laundry and feed the cat and dog.

Some of the other hospital mothers had husbands who came to the ward and told of feats of management with the house, the other children, the animals, and funny stories of small disasters.

"Are you sure you're all right?" Alice heard a wife ask, saying good-bye at the elevators.

"Don't worry." The man didn't look all right—hair spiky, pullover fraying out at the neck, growth of beard, toddler with wet pants and odd socks. "Stay as long as you have to."

Harry would come in after work with a list as long as his face of things that had gone wrong, and the inevitable question, "When are you coming home?"

Their son got better, but he was still weak. He couldn't play roughly with Harry as he had always done. He cried more and fell asleep on the sofa. He didn't want to go out with Harry for pizza.

"He's afraid he might throw up," Alice explained, but Harry said childishly, "You always take his side," as if Jeff were his brother, not his son, and Alice the mother of them both.

"Harry." Alice was very tired. "We could be in this together, if you'd only share it."

"I can't." He pulled her close and whispered into her hair, "I'm afraid."

"What of, love?"

"I have to pretend it isn't true. I want him healthy. I want my wife back. I can't cope with this."

"I love you." Alice sighed, because it was true. Why else were they still together?

Even when the father wants to be involved, he is usually working all day, and the wife must be the one who is there day and night on the ward, and loses her sleep, and makes the long journey to the clinic, and gives the pills at home, and holds the basin, and coaxes the child to eat, and watches for infection. She is a continuing part of the treatment. He can't be. When husbands are accused of withdrawing, it may be that they are feeling crowded out.

When Don's son got leukemia, he felt that he had "lost" this child. He had always been the teacher and the protector. "This is what we do now and this is how we do it." Little Don followed him around with a hammer and a paintbrush. He was glued to his father when Don was at home.

Don taught him to swim and play games. He took him walking in the woods and canoeing on the lake and camping on the mountain. He took care of his small problems and answered his questions and bandaged him when he fell. The child felt safe with him, and the father felt strong and necessary.

But leukemia . . . he couldn't save his son from that. He felt that he had let him down. The child was gone from him, into the world of doctors and nurses and pills that made him sick and too tired to do any of the hammer and paintbrush and canoe things.

Don's wife was very involved in the treatment. Don didn't want to be. He felt a failure because he couldn't be the kind of father he wanted to be. He did not think he could be a father at all. He wandered away in misery and did not come back.

Some marriages are not strong enough to stand the extra burden of a child's sickness or death. Crisis and tragedy can bring two people closer if they are already within reach, although grief must always be suffered acutely alone, which is its special torture. If the man and woman are already drifting apart, disaster isn't going to reverse the direction.

I have read that there is an eighty-five percent disintegration rate for marriages where a child is seriously or terminally ill, but I think that's far too high. The truth, in human rather than statistical terms, seems to be that through a crisis like childhood cancer, more families draw closer together than fly apart.

One mother had been to a lawyer to talk about separation.

"Then our son got cancer, and that was the end of separating. When it first hit us, those first few days of strangeness and terror, we had more sex than we had ever had or will have again. We clung together. We didn't talk much, but then we never had. He doesn't say much at the best of times."

One of the difficulties, as in all marriages, in all situations, is that women desperately want to talk, and men desperately want to shut up—or think they do.

The mother of a leukemia child wakes suddenly in the early hours. *What's wrong? What woke me? Billy?* And realizes that her husband is crying in the bed beside her, turned away.

"What is it?" She has never seen him cry.

"I thought you were asleep."

"You should have woken me."

"No."

"Tell me."

But he gets up and puts on his old dressing gown with the belt tied loose and low and pads off downstairs, and if she follows him, he is reading and she can't reach him.

Under the circumstances, a woman can get frustrated because a man doesn't want to talk, or will only talk about facts and opinions, never ideas and emotions. She knows from experience that whatever happens in life, it helps to talk about it. He doesn't know what's good for him, the poor dumb bastard.

When I pondered this to Dr. Selter who sees many parents of very sick children, he inquired alertly, "Why does she have this compulsion to reach him?"

I thought that was a shrink's twister—turning things back to the patient because you don't know the answer:

PATIENT (*weeping*): Nobody loves me.

DOCTOR (*attentively*): Why do you have this need to be loved?

But I see now what he meant. Whose good are we really talking about—his or hers?

Sometimes at Adele's parents' groups, a husband will start talking for the first time. He thinks he has gone there only for the educational part of the meeting. But when the speaker leaves and the discussion begins and feelings are unloaded, he may unexpectedly start to talk in a way he has never been able to do with his wife. In a curious way, it can be easier in a group and with people who don't know much about you and aren't involved with your life. Sometimes the wife and husband are able to tell each other things here that they never could alone.

Even if the talking never happens, those silent husbands are still often described as "a marvelous support; I could never have got through this without him."

Love and trust are there. The parents back each other up. The wife has other people to talk to, and she is turning that salient corner in marriage that leads to the revelation that she isn't going to change him and doesn't really want to.

Without much fuss about it, the family is bound together in the common cause of survival.

"Show me another of your noble spirits," I would ask John Truman, and having plenty to choose from, he would send me to see another brave survivor child, another staunch mother, another loving family who had, as many of them say, "just done what they could to get by."

Joey's family lives in Beverly, a fishing port north of Boston whose big harbor shelters hundreds of clean, bright pleasure boats and many more working boats that belong to the fishermen and lobstermen.

Joey's father has been going out after cod and flounder and lobster and crab all his life, taking his sons with him as they grew old enough. Joey's mother is one of my magical women, a steadfast survivor, understanding love and how to use it.

Joey is the youngest boy. When he was six, an age to start school and start fishing, he became very ill and was found to have a tumor on one kidney.

"A Wilms tumor," the doctor at Mass. General said. "One of the best cancers a child can have."

Joey is now thirteen. In the comfortable old shingled house near the harbor, the grandmother sits peacefully by the front window, one eye on the television, one on the street. In the kitchen, empty for once of relations and friends, Joey's mother Jean tells me about the day of the operation.

"I was in a fog, a world of my own. I hadn't asked the right questions and I hadn't listened to any answers. I hardly knew what was going on. I don't know what came over me. Terror, I suppose. I wasn't like myself.

"My sister and I, we wandered round that great hospital like lost souls. We saw a bulletin board. Current attractions. All the umpteen operations they were doing. There was Joey's name, it looked so strange. 'Nephrectomy,' it said.

" 'What's that?' I asked.

"My sister knew. Jeekers, I just about passed out. I'd thought it was just the tumor. But the whole kidney . . . a little kid like that. I was in shock.

"Afterward, it was worse, because Joey had all these tubes and needles in him. I was scared what my husband would think when he came in from fishing.

" 'Gee,' I says, 'Dick, it's happening to us.' We'd never had anything serious. I couldn't believe it.

"When we went home to get some things, the woman at the bank asked me, 'Did they get all the cancer out?'

" 'My kid didn't have that.' I couldn't use that word.

" 'Jean, he *did*.' My sister wouldn't let me stay in that fog where I was trying to hide.

"I stayed in the hospital and slept in the toy room. The nurses were so good, I can't explain it to you how wonderful everybody was. I was in the same boat as the other women.

My kid was very sick, but some of theirs were much sicker. We tried to help each other.

"Dick came in every night, although he despises driving to Boston. He hates it when he has to bring in the fish and lobsters to market, but there he was, every night. Joey and I would be at the window to see the red truck come around the corner from the river."

After Joey was discharged, they went to Dr. Truman's clinic to start the radiation and chemotherapy.

"The first time I saw Dr. Truman, I was shocked. I said to myself, *Jeekers, that man, so young and so handsome. What's he doing here?* I was crying like a fool because of what they told me Joey still had to go through and what could still happen. There was another mother there very distressed, several little kids—did they all have cancer?

"We got used to it somehow, my sister and I. She was like a post to lean on, jeekers, yes. She came in with us every day for a month, train and then bus, carrying Joey, we had to, because he was so weak from the radiation and the drugs.

"After a bit, Dr. Truman says, 'Hey, he can go to school.'

" 'Bald is beautiful,' we told Joey, but in the gym, his new wig fell off and the kids laughed, so we threw it away and got him those blue-striped railroad engineer's caps and he wore them all the time, glued to his head, indoors and out.

"The worst time came some months later when Joey was suddenly very sick, thin, he looked awful, vomiting, in great pain. We thought we were going to lose him. We thought, *Oh gee, the cancer's spread.* They had to open him up again and it was adhesions.

" 'Gee, if they hadn't operated,' Dr. Truman says, 'he could have died.'

"Oh, that was the worst thing. I was beside myself.

"One of my off days." She describes it placidly, as we look at the album of Joey pictures—fat and jolly, then

146

skinny, with eyes sunk in shadowed lids—at all stages of his pilgrimage.

" 'What next?' I says. I can't take any more, but then he got a bad infection in his leg from a splinter, because he had no immunity. They rushed him into the hospital again and he had a cast on that leg for months. The only thing he'd eat was chocolate pudding, so we used to mix his pills into that.

"A series of disasters. I thought we were being punished."

"Who by?"

"I dunno. God, I suppose," Jean says, without rancor.

Now Joey has been out since before dawn, winching in the lobster traps, putting in his small brown hand to pull out the muscular lobsters and measure them from the eye socket to the edge of the carapace, putting rubber bands around the cutter and crusher of the blindly waving claws, throwing back the undersize lobsters and the conch shells and spider crabs that get into the traps.

His father kicks off his boots on the back step and comes into the kitchen.

"Where's Joey?" Jean asks.

"Selling crabs down the dock."

Jean has been telling me what a great support Dick was to her and Joey, carrying on with his work at sea, but always there when they needed him.

His cake is ready in the oven at just the time he comes in. Sharing it with me, he jerks his head toward Jean and tells me, "*She* did it. I couldn't do much about it. I don't know about all the medical stuff. She took care of it all. I didn't do anything to help."

"That's not what Jean says. What about you driving the truck to the hospital every night?"

"Oh, sure. Who wouldn't?"

One of Joey's big brothers comes in from the boat, grabs something to eat without pausing, and goes on through to change his fishy clothes and go out. Various people come in and out of the house for various reasons. The kitchen fills, the way Jean likes it. Dick's mother has left the television and is rinsing mugs and swabbing about at the counters with a damp cloth.

Jean leaves someone to start the supper and takes me down to the harbor to meet Joey.

"He never talks about what he went through. He didn't at the time, never complained, never said much. At the hospital, they wanted him to see a psychologist.

" 'Oh my God,' my sister said, 'if we have one of *them* come to the house, everyone's going to think we're nuts. If we can't handle it ourselves, there's something wrong with this family.'

"We help each other. Friends too. In and out of the house all day. We've never had much, but we give to each other."

Among the glorious mess of masts and nets and crates and ropes, we leave the car in a pothole lined with broken clam shells and walk out to the end of Dick's pier. In a red boat called JEAN B, Joey is below us in a blue fisherman's sweater, hosing down the well deck of the big broad boat.

"Hey, Joey!"

He drops the hose and hops up onto the planking, a grinning, handsome boy with a flop of sticky, salty hair in his eyes.

"Show us what they did to you."

He flips up his sweater to show the enormous nephrectomy scar that practically cuts him in half.

"Shark got me." He flips the sweater down, jumps back into the boat, picks up the hose again, and goes on with his life.

Chapter TWELVE 🌿

$\mathcal{D}$r. Truman's respect for the parents of his patients extends to those who refuse treatment on religious grounds, or because they have their own different ideas about health care.

When this conflict of conscience and ethics and responsibility comes up, the doctors and the parents must both suffer, while the sick child, like a drummer boy caught out in no-man's-land, takes his chances between the two opposing beliefs.

The several cases where Jehovah's Witness parents refused permission for life-saving blood transfusions led to a 1944 Supreme Court decision that says that parents are free to make martyrs of themselves, but not to make martyrs of children too young to decide for themselves.

If the parents refuse a blood transfusion, which is often needed in the early stages of acute leukemia, the hospital will seek a court ruling at once. There is usually very little time. If it's after hours, the judge comes to the hospital and convenes court among the small furniture in the ward playroom, sometimes at two or three in the morning.

The crux of the decision is whether the doctor can prove that the treatment is essential and effective. Now that leukemia is in many cases curable, the judge will invariably order that the transfusion be given, as a necessary part of the treatment.

The parents lose. But they also gain.

However strong their religious convictions and taboos,

it is not their fault that events must go against that. They have done everything they can. They have obeyed their religious teaching, and now they have got to obey the law. Is it minimizing the sincerity of their faith to guess that it may be a relief that it's out of their hands? The conflict between spiritual conscience and parental love is over. It is all right for them to allow their child to get well.

In the autumn of 1977, there began the story of a small boy with leukemia that caused bitter distress to everyone concerned and a storm of publicity that made the tottery little figure of Chad Green, stumbling over the frozen snow ruts in his obliterating woolen hat, unbearably familiar on television and newspaper pages all over the United States.

When Chad was about a year and a half, he was taken to a hospital in Nebraska with a temperature of a hundred and six. Acute lymphocytic leukemia was diagnosed.

His parents were afraid of the standard drug treatment. Like many of us inexpert customers of modern medicine, they were wary of doctors and hospitals and the miracle drugs that they could not understand or control. Unlike most of us, who have to go along with it because it's the best we know, they refused to cooperate.

Chemotherapy to them was as threatening a word as cancer. Strongly religious Baptists, they would rather let Chad go to be in glory with God, they said, than suffer the ordeal of chemotherapy. They changed their minds— understandably, for who could stick to a decision like that while there was still some hope?—and treatment was started.

The Nebraska hospital was using cranial radiation at that time. To escape that, the Greens moved to a family house near Scituate, Massachusetts, and brought Chad to Dr. Truman in Boston.

Chad was now in remission, six weeks after diagnosis. He did not need radiation, which Mass. General was not using anyway, but needed continuing maintenance drugs for two or three years, with spinal injections to destroy any cancer cells in the central nervous system. He could visit the hospital clinic for intravenous and spinal drugs and take pills at home.

What were his chances?

At his age and with this type of "null cell" leukemia, a ninety percent chance of a year's remission, a seventy percent chance of two years without cancer, and at least a fifty percent chance of a complete cure.

If he were not treated?

"He will be dead in six months."

Dr. Truman often uses his seasoned parents to befriend new and untried families who are just coming warily into the system. He called Deborah, who lived in Scituate.

"I have a couple from the Midwest. Their son was diagnosed with ALL at the same age as David, and they're having trouble coping with chemotherapy. Can you help them?"

Deborah called Diana Green and they talked about Chad and about David's treatment and what it had done for him, and also about what he had gone through and what the parents had endured, for Deborah has learned from John Truman that it's better to lay out all the worst things that can happen. Then it's good when they don't.

Diana sounded negative.

"Come and see David."

"Well . . . I don't know."

When Deborah called again, Diana told her that Chad had a clinic appointment the next day.

"Want me to drive you in?"

"No, that's all right."

Her voice made Deborah ask, "Are you going to the clinic?"

"No."

"Please at least come and see David."

The Greens came reluctantly that evening, with Chad, the beautiful flaxen child, in a bright purple van. They were confused, hurt young people, Gerald a large shaggy man who worked as a welder, Diana a small attractive woman, brighter than her husband perhaps, but letting him take the lead.

David, off chemotherapy for about three years, was displayed, strong and lively, and the album of photographs dating from when he was diagnosed, through the illness to the end of the treatment, was shown. He was smiling in all of them.

"Most of the time, he wasn't sick. Chad can lead a normal life."

"With those chemicals in him?" Gerald had become rather blustery and defensive. "We've got other ideas. Natural substances. A new metabolic drug called Laetrile. I've read books and books."

"So have I," Dave said, "and they all point to chemo."

"Nobody's going to make my son a guinea pig."

Small hairs bristled at the back of Deborah's neck. "Look," she said. "David was a guinea pig for Chad."

"Nobody's gonna tell us what to do."

"I know it's devastating to hand over the life of your small child to someone," Deborah said carefully, with her fists still clenched. "But John Truman has devoted his whole life to saving children. He wants to save Chad."

But the Greens did not trust the doctor or the hospital or anyone who represented established authority. By the end of the visit, they were treating Deborah and Dave as part of the enemy establishment, and Dave, always so mild-mannered, was purple with suppressed anger.

But Deborah felt calmer. She called Dr. Truman in the morning.

"I think they'll be there."

Chad's chemotherapy continued. He was lucky. He did not suffer from the side effects as much as some children, but one drug gave him stomach cramps and another darkened his sunny nature enough to make the Greens ask the doctor again:

"What if we stopped the treatment now?"

A hundred percent certainty that the cancer would recur.

The Greens believed in the curative powers of prayer and a vegetarian diet and intensive vitamins. They were also under the influence of a local nutritionist who claimed to be able to diagnose cancer from saliva and to cure it by a meat-free diet with lemon juice, distilled water, minerals, and vitamins.

The Greens had faith in him. Who is to say that they were wrong? When your child is ill enough to die, you grab at any chance. You have to pin your faith on something. Most parents pin it on doctors. The Greens did not.

They insisted that the injections be stopped. Chad hated the needles as much as any child and added his screams, before, during and after, to those of the other little ones at the clinic, unlucky enough to be hit by cancer, lucky enough to be born in the years of knowledge and possible cure. Afterward, the Greens said, he was wild and uncontrollable, not a bit like his usual self.

All right. Instead of the injections, another pill could be added to the two already taken at home.

Plus our special diet.

The diet was of no value to the disease, but probably harmless.

Would the chemotherapy and the diet balance, or would they fight?

The doctor was sure of what he wanted. This was at least his hundredth child with acute lymphocytic leukemia. The Greens were still in an agony of indecision, but they did, that November, agree to go on with the drugs.

Dr. Truman asked Deborah to call the Greens again, but Diana would not speak to her.

In January the next year, Chad's white cell count was unexpectedly high, and Dr. Truman increased the dosage of the home drugs. To his surprise, Chad was worse on his next visit. He had a cold and fever. His liver was enlarged. There were pinpoint hemorrhages in the skin under his arms. Blood tests showed a recurrence of cancer cells.

Was he taking all the drugs?

Yes.

Regretfully, Dr. Truman had to explain to the Greens that a return of leukemia cells during chemotherapy is a very bad sign, probably fatal, and parents have the right to discontinue the drugs, which now may be useless.

All the parents to whom he had had to say that so far had chosen to go on trying. The Greens were the first to tell him to stop all treatment.

A bone marrow test would be needed.

No. The child had suffered enough.

The doctor reminded them again of the heart of the question: If Chad had relapsed while no longer on drugs, there was still a good chance of regaining remission. If he had relapsed while on the drugs, there was no chance.

And as the Greens were leaving, something made him ask: Had they *really* been giving Chad all the pills at home?

In the doorway, Diana turned and shook her head.

Which one had been stopped?

All of them.

Since how long?

Three months.

After four days of calling the Greens every day to urge them to resume treatment, since leukemia cells divide and multiply every four days, Dr. Truman had no choice but to get an order for temporary guardianship. In all the furor of abuse that was lavished for months upon the doctor and the hospital as enemies of freedom, it was largely unknown or ignored that they were not free either. A Massachusetts ruling decrees that in a life-or-death situation, a doctor is bound by law to go to court, if that is the only way to provide treatment.

That afternoon, a court-appointed guardian appeared without warning at the Greens' house and carried Chad back to the hospital.

The side effects from the chemotherapy were slightly worse this time, since he had to go back to very intensive treatment, but he did not suffer, and by April he was back in remission.

To the judge who presided at one of the hearings in what now became a long struggle for guardianship, he appeared to be a normal, healthy two-year-old. His ruling that Chad should remain in treatment was based on three premises: scientific evidence that with this type of leukemia, there was a substantial hope of at least five years of remission and even a cure; lack of evidence that the parents had a feasible alternative plan; and the duty of the State to protect a minor's right to life and to "substitute its judgment" to determine if that minor would choose or refuse treatment, if he were old enough.

That was when the publicity hit. This decision, which reversed another judge's earlier decision to return custody to the parents, started the storm that raged back and forth through and around the Chad Green story for the next year and a half and that made the family's life into public property.

Those reporters who were not hanging around the Greens' house in Scituate were camped out at Mass. General, hoping to feed into the popular desire to see omniscient doctors proved wrong, and the totalitarian structure of a huge established hospital defeated by the little people.

In America, doctors have been glorified into a cross between God and a magician. Having created that, it's fun to knock it down.

The Greens came to represent the little victims of the State. If they had been bizarre, cranky-looking people, with their wheat grass and chicken feet and coffee enemas and their declaration that Chad's relapse was only a detoxification phase after the chemical poisons had been cleansed by the special diet, they might have lost the sympathy of the people who fear freaky long-haired notions and have a sneaking suspicion that the ecologists are going too far. But when the publicity started, Gerald had been advised to shed some of his head and face hair and his cowboy boots and jeans, and he had even changed his purple van for a car. The Greens looked "normal" by all standards, and almost everyone was sorry for them.

Their fan mail grew. Every television station wanted an interview. The hospital received bundles of hate mail, and Dr. Truman hired an answering service to field the more paranoid calls.

During the weeks of court battles, while visiting nurses gave Chad his daily drugs and Diana Green took him to the clinic appointments—she and the doctor had agreed quite amicably to disagree—Gerald found a ready audience in the cynically salivating press and television reporters.

He offered some outdated statistics to show that Dr. Truman's testimony that Chad could be cured by drugs and would die without them was a "bunch of baloney." But if the child should die, he was widely quoted as saying, "at least he'll be going to a better place with God, where he won't suffer from poisonous drugs and needles."

Subpoenaing the Deity lost him a bit of sympathy in some quarters, and newspapers' Letters to the Editor used words like "superstition, ignorance, bigotry and/or opinionated idiocy," but this was counteracted by pictures of Chad with his wispy flaxen hair and his delicate face all smile and huge round eyes, and the parents' statement that chemotherapy made him like a wounded wild animal.

After a few of Gerald's denser pronouncements, Diana began to emerge from behind his bluster to be the one who was the spokesperson at the court hearings. Neat and articulate, emotionally appealing as the concerned mother, the Greens' advisors saw that she made a more acceptable advocate.

Deborah and Dave were both in court among the witnesses for the hospital, but the lawyers used only Deborah to match Diana as another concerned mother who could tell the story of a child with Chad's illness who was now officially pronounced cured, with no damaging after-effects.

From the witness stand, Deborah saw Gerald's face close in front of her in the courtroom, full of hate and anger. Shaking, empty of breath, afraid she would not be able to speak, her eyes found John Truman's face, pale and tired, with a nod for her. She knew that he had been hurt, not only by the Greens' condemnation of him as arrogant and cold, but because of his feeling for the little boy they would not allow him to save.

Outside the courthouse, one of the television reporters told her that the Greens had confided to him that the child they saw when they visited Deborah and Dave was borrowed for the evening, because David was already dead.

In September of that year, Dr. Truman happened to read in a newspaper that Chad was now healthy because he was receiving Laetrile. This controversial drug, made from apricot and peach stones, had been medically discredited as not only useless but dangerous, since it contains six percent cyanide, which in chronic poisoning could cause damage to the central nervous system, with possible blindness, deafness, and paralysis. An eleven-month-old girl in Buffalo had recently died of cyanide poisoning after eating five of her father's Laetrile pills.

The next phase of the legal war was not about chemotherapy, but about the Greens' "metabolic therapy." By midwinter the Laetrile, illegal in Massachusetts, had built up in Chad's blood the cyanide level of a heavy smoker, or an African chronically poisoned by cassava root. He was also being given enzyme enemas, which can damage the large intestine and spread bacteria to the blood stream, and doses of vitamin A large enough to risk hypervitaminosis and liver damage.

The four professional witnesses for the Greens, while admitting that Laetrile could not cure leukemia, claimed that it minimized the toxic effects of chemotherapy and was a placebo to make the patient feel better (like the 5 cc of sterile salt water we used to shoot into hypochondriacs when I was a nurse, which sent them off as blissfully as if it were morphine).

Remarking that since Chad was only three years old a placebo effect was doubtful, and that some of the Laetrile witnesses seemed to have a financial interest in its manufacture and sale, the judge ruled against the metabolic therapy, and the Greens took off for Mexico.

From the cancer clinic of Dr. Ernesto Contreras in Tijuana, Diana called their flight "a last, desperate, drastic act."

Eight months later, on August 11, she announced that Laetrile had cured Chad. "God is the healer, and Chad is healthy now."

Doctors in the United States had been saying that any success claimed for Laetrile was because the Mexican clinic used chemotherapy as well, but the Greens had stopped those pills in July, against the wishes of Dr. Contreras.

On August 14, Chad died in Tijuana.

It has never yet been established what caused his death. The Mexican undertaker embalmed his body before the post mortem, which hindered the findings of the private pathologist employed by the Greens. The only part of his report that he was allowed to release showed the presence of leukemia cells in the kidneys and liver and near the electronic system of the heart. An independent laboratory revealed that tissue samples he sent to them contained cyanide. Dr. Truman agrees that Chad could have died of an infection such as pneumonia but suspects that he died of cardiac rhythm disturbance due to the combination of leukemia cells and cyanide.

Leukemia, cyanide, infection—Chad had "gone home," the Greens said, and they would never come back to Massachusetts.

Eighteen months later, Judge Francis Keating was driving to work at the Plymouth District Court when he heard on his car radio that the Greens had returned to Massachusetts to face criminal and civil charges of contempt of court.

"In half an hour, Diana and Gerald Green will know their fate, when it is pronounced by Judge Keating."

How's that again? At the courthouse, he told the judge who had issued the original order forbidding the Greens to take Chad out of the state, "This is your case, not mine."

"I feel too strongly about them. I don't trust myself not to put them in jail."

The attorney general, quoting Dr. Truman's opinion that the child would probably be alive if left in his care, asked Judge Keating for a year in jail for the Greens.

The defense lawyer offered apologies on their behalf.

"Where are they?"

"They are not in court."

"Get them here."

Standing by the window, the judge watched Diana and Gerald Green come around the corner from the parking lot. It looked like a lynching. They could hardly walk in the middle of the mob of reporters who clutched at them, thrust microphones and cameras in their faces, and raced ahead of them to aim from the shoulder with their television guns.

The Greens came into the crowded courtroom with Bibles in their hands as big as encyclopedias. Gerald was silent. Diana spoke for them both. She apologized for the contempt of court. They had done what they thought was best for their child.

Did Mr. Green agree?

He agreed.

"I accept your apology," the judge told them. "I will find you guilty of contempt—this court does not make light of your offense—but any further punishment beyond what has been endured would be unfair."

The Greens looked at him, astounded.

"You have suffered enough," he said.

He cleared the court, but it was already clearing as the press and television people stampeded out with the Greens.

The case had lasted less than thirty minutes but it brought the judge more publicity and letters and phone calls than he had ever had in his judicial life, good or bad.

There were letters and Christmas cards from all over the country:

You have restored my faith in mankind . . .
Restored my faith in the law . . .
Thank you for your compassion . . .
God bless you for being a truly just judge . . .
Your face on TV showed you to be a very fair, believing man . . .

After a bit, the judge's wife wouldn't let him read any more of the letters out loud to her.

Judge Keating believed that he had done no more than anyone would have done with this couple who had lost their only child. When he had read the year before that the Greens would not return to Massachusetts for fear of a prison sentence, he had thought, *No one would put them in jail.* He was surprised now when other judges told him, "Don't be too sure. I would have put them away."

And there were cynics who suggested that perhaps he had done the Greens less of a favor than he thought. Suppose they had hoped to make the court a public villain as well as the hospital? Suppose they had secretly wanted, not to have done wrong and be forgiven, but to have the judge do wrong and hand them the final phase of their martyrdom?

In the retrospect of this sad, sensationalized story, which was a Roman holiday while it lasted, but is already retreating into the shadows of "Who was Chad Green?", perhaps the only people qualified to add the last words are the parents of other children with cancer.

"At the time, I thought they were brave. Now that my child has leukemia, I think they were cowards."

"We've had to go through it—why couldn't they? Why make heroes of them when the rest of us just go quietly through the horror of having to submit a child who's not very sick to the sickness and pain of the treatment?"

"Every chemical my child took was damaging to her body and could have killed her. But if she hadn't taken them, she would have been dead, like Chad."

"You do wonder, like they did—of course there are times when you wonder if it's worth it, because you see other children in treatment dying and you think, Is it right to put him through this when he might die anyway? I've wanted to say, 'No more chemo, no more radiation, no more destroying what's good along with what's bad.' But in the places they didn't radiate, his tumors reappeared."

"My child didn't suffer, and nor did Chad. He never vomited or lost his hair or bled. And he was curable. They robbed him of that. Parents don't have the right to make human sacrifices, any more than child-beaters do."

"But do we want the State to take over? The Greens were wrong, but they had a right to be wrong. Do we want to get like China, where neighborhood spies report who's not buying Tampax, and if you don't have a permit to be pregnant, they can haul you off for an abortion?"

"The doctor told me, 'Five years ago, when we didn't have these drugs, I'd have said you had the

right to take your son home. Now, if you tried to do that, I'd fight you all the way.' I felt glad that he cared so much about my child."

"The Greens were stupid."
"They had no guts."
"They were selfish."
"They ran away."

"If they really thought there was no hope, I can see trying every last thing, even Laetrile. I'd go to the ends of the earth."

When we first heard about the Greens, we were just starting into chemotherapy. Here we were, saying, 'It's our only hope.' Here the Greens were, saying, 'It's poison.' "

"I was afraid to agree to the treatment at first, but I knew that Chad's parents had tried something else and failed. That made it easier for me to accept. So when my child was in remission, I thought, 'The Greens did me a favor.' "

Chapter THIRTEEN 🌿

"**D**id they ever feel guilty about Chad?" Barbara wonders. "Their child could have lived. We did everything we possibly could for Brian, but I still feel this terrible guilt that I let him down at the end."

Barbara is one of the mothers who worked to get the Rest Inn Retreat house going for Mass. General families. In all the time she spent with her son in the hospital—a hundred and eight days in a year and a half—a house like that would have given her the sanctuary she has now helped to provide for mothers of the future.

Hodgkin's disease, cancer of the lymphatic system, is ninety-five percent curable, but it sometimes goes undiagnosed for too long. When Brian's new Christmas shirts would not meet at the collar, everyone thought it was because he was in training for football, which needs a husky neck or your head will roll off.

No blame to the family. Who ever expects a strong, muscular fifteen-year-old to have cancer?

When the baseball season rolled inexorably around, Brian took up running to cover his disappointment in not being picked for team training. He also covered the fact that running made him dizzy and breathless and sick, until one night he threw up his supper into his plate.

"Brian!" This boy was never ill.

"It's okay. It happens all the time."

"All the *time?*"

"I've always managed to make it to the bathroom. Sorry."

163

He got up, knocking over his chair, and groped at the doorway.

"What's the matter with your eyes?"

"When I'm dizzy, I can't see straight."

"Is that what went wrong with the baseball?"

"Yeah. Couldn't see the ball."

Their local doctor could not see Brian for two weeks. England is not the only country where you have to be healthy enough to live long enough to see a doctor. When he finally got to the Boston hospital and the test determined that he had Hodgkin's, they removed his spleen. All used cells pass through the spleen to be cleaned, so you can't risk a cell with Hodgkin's contaminating others. But because it was part of the lymph system, they could not remove the mass in his chest that had made those Christmas shirts too small four months ago, and which was now as big as a football. It was pressing on his heart and lungs, pushing everything out of place. All the time he had been trying to play baseball, to run and lift weights, breathless and dizzy, this thing had been growing there.

They thought of it as "the thing." It was treated with chemotherapy to see if it would shrink enough to be radiated without harming anything else. When the mustard gas burned out his veins, a whole variety of new drugs was tried. He was in charge of his own treatment, keeping the complicated chart of his pills and his trips to the clinic. He was so unnervingly brave, sensible, and grown up at fifteen that it was almost a relief when he broke down— just once—and was an angry and frightened child. When he went back to being brave and sensible and grown up, his parents and the doctors respected him even more, having seen what he fought with close below the surface.

In the kitchen, he had suddenly taken a pen and slashed DEATH IS GREAT! across the treatment chart and cried and screamed and beat on the walls and yelled that he would rather die than take another pill.

He got on the train and went to Boston to tell Dr. Tru-

164

man that and came home to the chart and the pills. He managed his treatment like a business, and before the end of summer he went back to his beloved football training again.

"Please, not till—" Barbara began, but the doctor had already agreed. One of the hardest times for all the mothers is when they are not allowed to mother.

It was nine-fifteen on Saturday, September 2, 1978 (all the parents remember exact dates, times, and days of the week). It was the long Labor Day weekend, the last holiday weekend of the summer. Barbara and Matthew were painting the kitchen. Brian was out at the playing field. No, he wasn't. There were his bare feet on the stairs, and his voice, rather faint, from the doorway.

"I finally made a decision."

"About what?" Standing on a chair to paint a cupboard door, Barbara did not look around.

"No football," he mumbled.

Happy to hear this, Barbara looked around at the stranger standing miserably in the doorway. His face and head had blown up like a pumpkin. He could hardly breathe. Barbara drove him to the hospital, still wearing her overalls splattered with white paint.

The radiation began to burn Brian's stomach into ulcers. He couldn't eat. Powerful new drugs were started, but he never had more than a few bearable weeks at a time. He was still doggedly hopeful, desperate for life, pulling his family along in his belief that he could fight this; but at each improvement, it was not long before he was knocked back down, like the frog in the well, to brace himself again for new surgery, a new cycle of drugs.

He had lost weight alarmingly. If he could not eat because of the drugs, he would not be strong enough to take them. A gastrointestinal specialist was sent in to discuss supplementary feeding: a cold mogul who treated him like a child instead of the man he had become, in charge of his own case.

"They tell me you want to gain weight. Why?"

"I'm down sixty-five pounds."

"You're almost the right weight for your age." The GI man looked at the boy on the bed, with his hairless skull and angry swollen face, too large for the bony body.

"Listen to this," he said, as if he had learned it in a textbook on therapy for terminal adolescents, which perhaps he had. "You have to want to live."

For once, Brian let his mother answer. After she had chased the doctor out of the room, she yelled at him down the corridor never to come near her son again.

When Dr. Truman came to be complained at, Brian asked him calmly if he could have a tube inserted through the abdominal wall into his stomach and feed himself through that.

He did, for five months, pouring into himself through a funnel four thousand calories of milky fluid, like baby food. He gained his weight, went back to school, and cured quite a few students of their drug habit when they saw what drugs had done to him.

After he was knocked back again, Barbara's sister came for a night. She was going to the West Coast and Brian did not want her to know how ill he was. He asked some friends to come around, to make it look as though he were all right.

When she left for the airport, he could not get back up the stairs to bed.

When I brought him to the hospital that night, I knew we were not going to bring him back. I think he probably wanted to die at home, but he didn't say so. He knew that I was afraid I wouldn't know how to help him, and he knew, because he knew everything about his illness, that his dying could be a terrible struggle.

It was. He struggled to live. He never gave up, but at the end the tumor took over everything. It was

*choking him, his mouth and throat were dried up and
burning with sores because he couldn't swallow. He
was suffocating.*

*When he died, I was out in the hall, because I
couldn't stand to see him suffer anymore. I can't forget that. I ask myself still: Why did God give me the
courage to be with him every minute of the way, but
then I failed him at the end?*

I have no answer.

*Sometimes I ask myself: Was he upset that I wasn't
there? It tortures me that I can't ever know. Doctors
say that people at the point of death are already un-
conscious and moving on beyond the room in which
they die, but when I went out for the last time, half
an hour before he died, he knew what was happening.
He was so angry that he had lost. The look on his
face—I'll never forget.*

*I don't think now about all the pain. I forget that
now. I think about all the things we loved and looked
forward to, his ideals, the hopes we all had for each
other. But I don't forget that I couldn't stay with him
when he died. Was he angry with me because I wasn't
there?*

I have no answer.

Georgina's mother had not wanted another baby. Then
she didn't want it to be born on a day not convenient for
her. Then after the baby had been born early by induced
labor, she didn't want a daughter.

When Georgie was three, she developed a treatable
form of leukemia, achieved a remission, which did not
surprise the doctor, but suffered an early relapse, which
did not surprise her mother, who had never been hopeful.

Knowing how steeply the chances had dropped, no one
expected Georgie to live long, but the child produced what
doctors call the Lazarus Syndrome—recovery and excep-
tional survival for many years.

Ten years later, she relapsed again, with a more lethal form of the disease. The new diagnosis was virtually a death warrant.

Georgie knew this and did not know it; a more intensive version of the way in which we all know we shall die, without completely believing it.

"As long as I'm not dead, there's a chance I'll survive," she told Max, who was her boyfriend at the hospital, another teenager under sentence of death.

As it got closer and they allowed themselves to drop the illusion and talk about the truth, it was without abandoning the truth of what they still had.

"While I'm alive, I'm alive," Georgie said, "and I'm going to live till the moment I die."

But when she was very ill, bleeding internally and suffering, she would talk about dying as a release.

"Do what you have to, darling." Her mother, very close to Georgie now, had prepared herself long before for her daughter's death.

"No more pain. I could die in peace," Georgie said rather wistfully, as if it were something she might like, but might not get.

After her last case discussion, the doctor who had been with her for years walked away from the group with some excuse, that perhaps he did not recognize as an excuse, not to tell Georgie that she was dying now.

"Am I dying?" She put her direct question to his younger associate.

"I think so."

She asked to be taken home, and within twenty-four hours, she died, without a struggle, in peace.

Afterward, the younger doctor suffered greatly and was afraid of what he saw as his own power—he had said, "You are dying," and she went away and died. He was also uneasy, as most doctors are, at the possibility that people may have some control over their own death, when it seems that the doctor does not.

The mother's guilt was more complicated. In that later time when emotions quiet down and the thinking starts, the struggle for the survivor became, "Was it permission to die we gave her . . . or an order?

"When I knew I had to prepare myself for Georgie to die, was I really only preparing myself . . . or was I writing her off?

"If you don't want a child at the beginning, can you ever make up for that later? This child was born before she was ready, because I'd selfishly set my date and I made the doctor keep it. Was that the beginning of her dying?"

The unanswered questions remain.

So does the image of sweet smiling Georgie, her shining eyes undimmed and her delicate face pricked into the flush of fever, on the hospital teaching film she helped to make before her death. Max is with her, although he did not expect to be with her for long. He always thought he would die first.

After Georgie's death in early December, he said that he would live through Christmas. On New Year's Day, he stopped his blood transfusions and all his drugs, and died five days later.

How do you talk to someone so young about dying?

They usually know the truth, even before they are told. If they have not talked about it, it could be because they are trying to protect you. So the way for someone close to them to talk about it is no more complicated than simply to talk about it. With honesty, and an encompassing assurance of love, and a concentration on the feelings of the dying boy or girl, not on your own.

To say "I can't bear it" or "I need you—don't leave me" is a natural expression of love; but the child is already miserably aware of causing great pain and sorrow. He doesn't want that rubbed in. He is the only one who has the right to say "I can't bear it," and that is the one thing the young hardly ever say.

If the family can promise, "We'll be all right. We'll survive. We'll go on," that leaves him free to die, if he must. That may be the last thing they can do for him.

For so long, they have fought and hoped and concentrated with him on the struggle to strengthen him against the disease. Sometimes when they are exhausted, they may be too pessimistic. Sometimes if he feels rotten, they may be too bracing. In this outlandish situation, there persists at least one familiar maxim for parents: You can't always do it right.

Nurse Kathy, who has listened to many adolescents on the ward talking to her about death and fear, has learned that each of them has their own way of going about it. Each younger person's way of living is unique to them, and so is their style of dying. You have to respect that and listen and watch for what they want.

If a nurse or a counselor comes to them at a set time with set ideas about what should be discussed and what feelings should be explored—"You're feeling angry. It's important to let the anger out"—teenagers will be turned right off. If they say "What's the use?" or something that sounds like despair, they can also be turned off by a therapeutic "Do you want to talk about it?"

"Tell me" is better.

Some children never talk about their death or their feelings at all.

Ann remembers: "Jimmy got very withdrawn toward the end. He'd always been one for making funny jokes. Even when he was quite sick, he'd fool about with Sue and Cindy, and if we had to wait for Dr. Truman in his office, Jimmy would have his feet up on the desk when the doctor came in and his arms folded, and he'd say, 'Well now tell me, young man, what's your problem?'

"When he stopped joking and turned his head away on the pillow when anyone came into the room, that's when I knew that he knew."

Jan and her son Paul never talked together about the most important thing of all.

"Looking back on his death, I see now by things I remember of what he said and how he behaved that toward the end he did know. Why couldn't we talk? I regret that so much. I've learned since then that you have to say what you're feeling, but at the time I was terrified. I didn't know what to say to myself, so I had no idea what to say to Paul.

"Thank God I was there when he died. Thank God we had him at home. He refused to have a hospital bed. He lay on his sofa there, right by the door. He could look out at the street, and he saw everyone who came in.

"Everyone was there, family and friends. My parents came from Florida. On that last day, when we had to eat something, my father went out and got clams. Paul got off his sofa. He could hardly walk, and he was in terrible pain, even with the morphine, but he went and sat on a chair and ate a clam.

"I had to go to the hospital for some tests for myself. When I got back, Paul said, 'Mummy, are you all right? What did they do?' Fifteen minutes later, he died. He waited for me to get home."

Kathy nursed a special boy who was in and out of Burnham 4 for three years. José had no mother, so Kathy and the other primary nurse became his mother. Kathy knew he was going to die, and perhaps professionally she knew she shouldn't get too close, but she is a gentle, loving woman as well as an experienced nurse.

When she went on vacation for two weeks, she left José active and fairly well. When she came home on a Sunday evening, another nurse called her and said, "If you want to see José alive, you'd better come in now. I think he's waiting for you."

He was. Kathy went to the hospital, and he died later that evening.

Kathy went to his funeral. "It helps the family when the nurse can do that. It proves that their child was special, and the hospital has been their life for so long, and the nurses are their close friends. It's hard for them to cut that off suddenly. Then you don't see them anymore. But about six or eight weeks later, they come back to the ward. Just once. They walk the halls, look at the child's old room, bring toys for the playroom, go over the history of the illness and its ending with the nurse. They haven't got over the death, of course, but they're out of the pit and beginning to take hold of life again. Part of their transition from tragedy is to go back and see the people who went through it with them."

Krissie is dying. The tumors that have come back into her lungs are now so many and so large that even with constant oxygen there is not enough lung tissue left to make use of it. She is gasping for breath. She will die of not breathing. Laura and Tom can only watch and wait and pray that it won't be too long, and tell her, "It's all right. Let go. You can go."

Not much more than a year ago, she said casually, "My leg hurts a bit. I think I've pulled a muscle." She was rehearsing for the *Nutcracker* ballet, leaping about like a colt, running in a cloud of breath along the icy roads at the outer end of Cape Cod, excited and noisy and temperamental and awkward, sensible and infantile, because she was fourteen.

The impatient harvester selects his victims carefully and gathers them greedily, just before they are ripe.

Stop that. That goes against what I rationally believe about the random chance of cancer. But when a child is dying, you are not thinking rationally.

She had to go through all that pain, and that terrible five-hour operation for the lung tumors and the amputation, and the torment afterward of the phantom leg. She faced life bald, skinny, anorexic, and coughing, with one leg and one jointed pipe covered with molded foam rubber, limping more than necessary, almost as if she wanted people to know that something was different.

172

She is dying in her room at home in the spring, but I remember her on the high bed at the Boston clinic, looking out through the big window onto the winter mess of dirty ice and snow and the frozen rubble of builders who have abandoned one of the new extensions that the hospital keeps crowding into its tiny nineteenth-century space between the river and the city buildings.

"This is my bed." Krissie lies back with the tubing running into the bandage that secures the needle in her bony wrist, her two different legs stuck out straight, identical in narrow jeans, wig a little crooked, with chopped bangs and a flyaway clump over one ear.

With a funny grimace, she explains, "When I come for my chemo, no one else has this bed."

She is queenly, childish, joking, anxious as she lies on the high narrow bed, receiving in her bloodstream the crusader chemicals that are not going to save her.

Chapter FOURTEEN

Krissie could not be saved because the cancer that started in her leg had metastasized extensively in her lungs. But an increasing number of children with leukemia who don't maintain a remission with chemotherapy are being saved by bone marrow transplants.

A transplant is no longer experimental. Although there are risks, it is approved as effective treatment after a dangerous relapse. The only reason more patients don't have one is the difficulty of finding a matching donor.

The prime risk of bone marrow transplants is graft-versus-host disease. Unlike other transplants, it is the grafted marrow that rejects the host body, rather than the other way around. The closer the match—the best being an identical twin, then a sibling—the less the risk.

Research programs are moving toward finding the key to eliminating the cells that do the rejecting, to widen the number of possible donors for any patient. One of these programs, undertaken by Dr. Elizabeth from Dr. Truman's clinic, is partly funded by the money Bert and Tobey raised in memory of Charley, who died before he could have the last chance of a bone marrow transplant.

Megan, another of Dr. Truman's small patients, was able to have that chance.

At the start of her illness, the doctor had told her mother, Beryl, "Megan will do just fine. She's the best age, with the best type of leukemia, and we caught it in time."

But she did not do just fine. She lost her remission. The

cancer cells were back, and although new and stiffer treatment was to start, Beryl got the negative impression that she was being asked to take part in a countdown. Her daughter was not going to get well.

The memory of this makes her more sympathetic to the Greens and their desperate search for alternative treatments for Chad. She took Megan to a chiropractor, read books, talked to everyone with a theory, and used natural foods and minerals to build the child up for the next assault of drugs.

Dr. Truman said cautiously, "Well, let me see whether I agree with those things."

"I've already done them. I'm not going to sit back and watch my child die."

Beryl was angry and exhausted and very lonely. After she spent all day at the hospital, a two-hour drive each way; collected Dana, the younger girl, from someone else's house and tried to pay some attention to her; and got a fretful, sick Megan into bed and held the bowl while she threw up her supper, her young husband would come home from work and want her to go out to dinner, the movies, dancing, "like we used to."

"Kevin—even if we could afford a babysitter . . ."

She didn't want to hear about his work, and he didn't want to hear about her day with Megan. There is a jaded air about that statement, because it is common to many marriages, but Beryl felt uniquely alone with the pain and terror of the illness, and the guilt and depression that all leukemia parents know, and the feeling of being turned inside out and having all your energy scraped away.

It was only when they were finally able to talk—it was either talk or separate—that she discovered that Kevin had been smothering his unhappiness and fear because it was the only way he could hold together. He couldn't work to support his family if he had Megan on his mind all the time, so he pushed her under and left Beryl to do everything alone, because he knew she could.

It was a year before they came toward each other with

honesty and glued the family back together. Without that, they might never have been able to go through the four-month ordeal of the transplant.

"It's a devastating thing," Dr. Truman told them. "A drastic form of treatment." A transplant means killing all the patient's bone marrow by drugs and radiation before replacing it with cancer-free marrow from the donor.

Megan had relapsed again. There was not much time to decide. Dr. Truman could not make the decision for them. He could only describe the transplant and urge them to get a second opinion.

The second opinion said, "Two percent chance now with drugs. Thirty percent with a transplant. You have no choice."

The third opinion said, "Here's your gamble. A transplant can cure her in months, or kill her. But chemotherapy can kill her too."

Beryl and Kevin asked each other, "How can we put her through it?"

"How can we let her die without trying everything?"

The most likely donor is always a brother or sister, and Megan's younger sister Dana came out of the tests a perfect match.

They couldn't ask her. She was only three. They could only tell her, "You're going to do something for Megan that nobody else in the world could do."

Mass. General does not yet do transplants. Sidney Farber clinic at Boston's Children's Hospital can only do two or three at a time and had no room for Megan. Beryl and Kevin had been talking to transplant units in different cities, hearing different things and being put on waiting lists, while Megan went downhill, until Seattle called them back and said cheerfully, "Be here next week!"

The apartments in which families live during treatment at the Fred Hutchinson Cancer Research Center are only a short walk away from the clinic, which is just as well, since it rains a lot in Seattle. This family settled in for four months, three thousand miles away from home.

The start of the adventure was discovering what an extraordinary place they had chosen, or been chosen by, with a closely integrated staff that pays as much attention to how you feel as to how you are.

"How do you feel?" has become the standard idiotic question of those who gather the news, thrusting a microphone into the shattered face of a woman pinned under an overturned car, or a cabinet member dodging out of court after a conviction for embezzlement or public obscenity, or the father of a psychotic gunman holed up in a bank with two live hostages and one dead one. Even if anyone answers they don't listen. They just need to ask the question, to show they are part of in-depth, eyewitness noos.

But at the Hutchinson Institute, when they ask "How do you feel?" they mean physically, mentally, and emotionally, and they want to know.

After more than a year as a hospital mother, Beryl was pleased to find herself being treated as an intelligent equal by everyone from the top doctors to the floor polishers, and even by the young men who came up from the depths with little baskets of test tubes to take blood, usually the most enigmatic acolytes in any temple of healing.

Everyone appeared to have limitless time to stop and talk. The whole family felt cherished and important. Suggestions and ideas were greeted seriously as useful reinforcements, not uninformed criticism.

Beryl had always taught Megan, young as she was, that thoughts and emotions can affect what happens to your body, and that however ill you are, it's not just the doctors, but you yourself who can help. The hospital reinforced this, and therapists prepared Megan for the ordeal psychologically as well as physically, teaching her relaxation and breathing techniques to overcome pain, as if she were a woman going into labor.

When she had to have surgery to insert the indwelling catheter that would carry the transplanted marrow through the cephalic vein and the vena cava to the heart, Beryl asked if she could have a local anesthetic because of the risk to her lungs just before the transplant.

"She'd be the youngest child to have a Hickman line put in without a general."

"I think she can take it."

"I can take it"—Megan was afraid, but deathly courageous—"if you stay with me."

While they injected zylocaine and cut down through the thin dry skin lying too loosely over the collarbone and threaded the tube under the skin and into the vein, Beryl stroked the child, breathed in a pattern with her, and told her stories until the line was stitched in and taped and the doctors and nurses were exclaiming how proud they were of Megan and inviting other staff to come in and view this heroine and be proud of her too.

On Dana's fourth birthday, she gave her sister Megan her unique gift. They put her to sleep and then took about seventy-five aspirations of her plentiful bone marrow with its vital "stem" cells that create themselves and don't die, from the spongy top and back of the pelvic bones—the prime factories for blood cells.

Meanwhile, to destroy all Megan's leukemia cells and the element in which they grew, every marrow cell in her body had to be wiped out. She was given the powerful drug Cytoxan and radiation for four hours, greater than the minimum lethal dose that was established after the experience of Hiroshima. The radiation had to be stopped every ten or fifteen minutes when she vomited.

The mother and father took turns being with Megan, who was suffering, weeping, vomiting, totally annihilated, and Dana, who had gone into the adventure healthy and placid and was coming out of the anesthetic sick and sore and screaming with rage.

The marrow to be grafted was treated and spun to get rid of foreign substances as quickly as possible. With none of her own now, Megan would die without it.

The vital part of the whole day's work was so deceptively simple. An intravenous stand, burettes, clips, clear tubing going into Megan's chest, and the innocent plastic bag hanging up like an ordinary blood transfusion, bestowing the gift of life, drop by gentle, bright red drop.

Dana had recovered by the end of the day, apart from soreness and stiffness when she walked. It would take two weeks for her transplanted marrow to graft into Megan, the time of greatest danger from graft-versus-host disease, which accounts for most of the transplant deaths.

The nursing is intensive and skilled. Many of the nurses have been there a long time, partly because of the rewards of the work, and partly because they enjoy higher status than in other hospitals, where the doctor is king. At the Hutchinson, the nurses are trusted for decisions and opinions because they know more than many of the doctors, who are only here to train and move on.

Megan's special nurses took care of her parents too when she became very ill and they were afraid that she would die, like other patients they saw who had died of liver damage from the battle between graft and host, going on respirator machines, not coming off them.

Megan's battle was mostly in her skin, inside and out. She had a rash all over, and her intestines and throat were raw. Her whole body, already scorched by the radiation, was consumed by burning and itching, inside the ears and eyelids, the whole mouth. It was a long time before she could swallow. She was on fire.

But there were patients whose rashes blistered and split like third-degree burns on the skin and through the whole digestive tract. Five people died when they were there, four of them teenagers. But many more walked out, with the new marrow integrated and making healthy blood cells, and Megan was one of them.

When I first met Megan much later, breathing heavily into her dollhouse with a red calico kerchief on her bald head, she had been a year in remission and had just come off all drugs. She had been given a sixty percent chance of maintaining the remission without a relapse.

Beryl tells me, "I used to think ahead, ahead, always ahead, and work myself up about tomorrow and next month and next year. But there's nothing you can do about all that. There is something you can do about today.

"I don't go around thinking, *My child might die.* I think, *My child is alive today; my child is alive at this moment,* which is more than most people ever think about, and so they miss that present pleasure."

Dana, who was going to be five, got up from a nap irritable, flounced with a flushed face and sticky hair into the room where Megan and her friend were playing peacefully, and started wrecking things.

All three of them fought and yelled. Megan and Dana were enraged with each other for two minutes and then forgot. It was a very ordinary family scene. Megan was alive *today*.

The news has just come through that Jill, whose chronic myelocytic leukemia would eventually accelerate out of control without the chance of a bone marrow transplant, is able, like Megan, to have that chance.

When Jill's astronomical white cell count had been brought down enough for her to think and understand clearly without the dizziness and confusion, she began to go around her neighborhood telling everyone—the hairdresser, the dentist, people in stores—"I have leukemia," because she thought they could read it on her face.

When they looked shocked, she said, "Oh, you mustn't worry," comforting them as she had comforted Kim on the ward in her motherly way. "I'm going to get better."

When her white cell count was down to twenty thousand, all the family came in for blood tests, her mother and father to see if they could give blood for transfusions. Her father, Tony, was convinced that his blood would match and that he would be the bone marrow donor, because he and Jill are so close, but parents hardly ever match. Everything depended on Jill's seven-year-old sister Jodi.

The test results have just come in. Jodi is a match and can donate life to her sister. Both girls know what is going to happen in a few weeks, but neither realizes its importance. Jodi wants to know, "Will I get toys?" Jill has always believed she is going to get better anyway.

Because her form of leukemia is so rare in children and the situation so critical, she has been picked by the chief specialist at Sidney Farber clinic, and the transplant will be done in Boston.

After Jodi's bone marrow is grafted into her, she will have to spend three or four months in a sterile bubble as an extra precaution against infection. For now, she and Jodi and Paula and Tony are going off on a ten-day cruise to the Caribbean to get away from "the other life" into which they were catapulted when Paula innocently showed her doctor a large swollen bruise inside Jill's upper arm.

A few months after they come back, Jill tells me, she will be able to go around telling everyone, "What did I tell you? I don't have leukemia anymore."

Jill's rare type of leukemia responds very well to bone marrow transplants, but for others, according to Dr. Truman, the success rate of transplants is still disappointing.

"The present looks a little cloudy," he says, "but the future holds some bright promise.

"At the moment, the general picture for marrow transplants hasn't improved. When you consider how many children have leukemia and how many do have relapses, it's remarkable how comparatively few transplants are done in this country. A lot of parents won't submit their child to this truly difficult and trying procedure and the risks that follow it. It can be so bad that many people prefer to choose the risk of death.

"One of my families has just faced this choice. The little girl's disease has recurred. She doesn't have compatible siblings, but she could possibly have an auto transplant— her own bone marrow drawn off and cleaned of cancer cells.

"The parents have talked to me very openly. They've discussed it with doctors at Sidney Farber and visited the transplant unit there and talked to a couple of young patients. Now, weighing all the things their child has been through already and the prospect of the ordeals that would lie ahead for her, they've chosen not to do it. I think that's a very courageous decision, more courageous perhaps than going ahead. It's been made completely for the child, not for themselves.

"I was totally unable to advise them which way to go. I could only assure them that whichever way they chose would be equally right. There is no right or wrong in this decision. There is just—you do it or you don't do it.

"That's with chronic lymphocytic leukemia. In the myelocytic type in its chronic phase, I'd advise anyone to do it. It has a far better track record. The myelocytic leukemias are a more honorable foe. If they're going to relapse, they stand and are counted in short order. The lymphoblasts lurk like guerrillas waiting to attack, a dishonorable and sneaky foe. Lymphoblasts can be eclipsed and in hiding for years and then suddenly reappear. But myeloblasts are out in the open and far easier to eradicate.

"The cure rate for bone marrow transplants with lymphocytic leukemia is no more than one out of four. With myelocytic it's much higher, about two out of three. Something in my mind says that when a child's chances are better than fifty-fifty, I feel happy about a transplant. When they're less, I feel sad about it. Until the chances for lymphocytic leukemia get to be better than fifty-fifty, I feel rather stand-offish about it.

"Auto transplant, or autologous transplant, subjects the child to the same difficult procedure, but the problems and

182

risks afterward are different. Because you're not putting in foreign material, the risk of graft-versus-host disease doesn't exist.

"Even if graft-versus-host doesn't kill the patient, it can leave them in a sad middle state, neither failure nor success, neither life nor death, but an awful condition that in animals is called runt disease. Chronic diarrhea, chronic bad skin, chronic liver disease, malnutrition, hair loss. It's like permanent radiation sickness.

"With auto transplants there are no chronic after-effects. More research is being done on things like the best time to harvest and freeze the patient's marrow. Basic scientists are working on nicer, more thoroughly successful techniques for getting rid of all the cancer cells, in the marrow and in the whole patient. The day will come when we will automatically harvest and store the patient's own marrow as soon as they gain their first remission.

"The future has some very bright moments. There is the possibility of transplants from siblings or unrelated donors who are not perfectly matched. Different immunological manipulations will diminish the risk of graft-versus-host disease by getting rid of those cells that become the graft that rejects the host—the T cells.

"And we now have the new computerized tissue-typing registry that has been developed. At the moment, only this country and the U.K. feed into it, but eventually it may be possible to discover a person anywhere in the world whose tissue typing matches the leukemia patient. There's an ethical problem here, though. Blood donors—potential marrow donors—don't know they're being tissue typed. They come in to offer blood and agree to donate white cells and platelets. During that process they are tissue typed. Is it entirely ethical for someone from another country to call and ask them, 'Would you be willing to be a donor of bone marrow for a dying patient?' That places extraordinary stress on someone who didn't know they were getting into this in the first place, and who now finds that the information on their blood has been made available not only in their own country but in someone else's.

"How can you say no to a dying child? Is it fair to put someone on the spot like that? On the other hand, if the dying child is yours, should you be denied access to what could be life-saving information?

"No doubt in the end people will be asked about tissue typing when they give white cells, like asking whether you want to donate organs when you get your driver's license. And the registry people will have to go back to those thousands of names already in the computer and ask them if they'd be willing to have their tissue-typing information released.

"Part of the transplant promise lies with the immunologists, in the development of antibodies that are more lethal to cancer cells, or more specific in killing the cells that cause graft-versus-host disease. I have to say that it looks like a glorious future.

"That's realistic, but sometimes articles about new or improved cancer treatments in the papers and interviews on television are much too optimistic. They raise hopes that can't be fulfilled, and that's dangerous. The press follows the science and medical publications with a microscopic lens. Every Thursday, the third item on the television morning news will be about some latest advance in medical science. That's how you know it's Thursday. Press releases from *The New England Journal of Medicine* aren't allowed until Thursday, after its subscribers have got the *Journal* in the mail, so they won't be caught napping by patients who ask, 'Did you hear what it said on TV about this new breakthrough for cancer?'

"So every Thursday a media mountain is made out of what is usually a molehill. Most scientific advances are a series of tiny incremental molehills. But the press needs to create big news, and so they're always discovering a holy grail when in reality what they've got is just a Styrofoam cup. Physicians are to blame too. It's flattering to have all three networks with their floodlights turned on you while you discuss your latest data on prostatic cancer and the use of an exciting new fungus to defeat it.

"I've read articles that claim there are twice as many leukemia cures today as there were three years ago. That could be statistically true, but it's because more children have now completed their chemotherapy and have been in remission for at least four or five years—long enough to be called cured.

"It's not because chemotherapy, to the best of my understanding, is one fig better than it was ten or fifteen years ago, at least for ALL. But the good news is that the promise of a proportion of cures held out in the sixties has been fulfilled. The discouraging thing is that the increment of improvement has not continued.

"We went from zero to fifty percent between 1966 and 1972. The logical next thing would be to go from fifty percent to eighty and then from eighty to ninety and a hundred. That's not true, except for the progress in myelocytic leukemia, which represents about twenty percent of all childhood leukemias.

"So. A promise has been fulfilled, but has only been improved on by a very small amount. The future of transplants looks good, but I feel far less enthusiastic about the future of chemotherapy. It's been around for quite a while, but not much seems to be happening, and the treatment hasn't changed. We seem to have come about as far as we're going to. I predict that one day we'll look back on the eighties with the same sense of bemusement with which we read old medical journals, or Thomas Mann's *The Magic Mountain* and the primitive treatment of tuberculosis. 'Why did we do that?' we'll ask. 'On what basis? How antique.'

"Perhaps chemotherapy will eventually become outdated by some entirely new treatment we don't even know about yet. If it's chemical warfare of any sort, it's going to be vastly different from what we wage now. And it may not be chemical warfare at all. Harvesting, enlisting the help of the body's own defense system will ultimately prove to be much more valuable.

"Immunologists may be able to develop more sensitive means of finding cancer cells, so they will be able to spot them when they're smaller. Blood tests can recognize specific antigens that are characteristic of cancer cells. You don't have to see the darn things yourself. Liver cancers, for instance, have become simpler to spot when they're tiny and easier to remove completely.

"It may be that the future is prevention. Even if only a modest amount of cancers could be prevented . . . I don't know. One reads that eighty percent of cancers are environmentally induced, but I doubt it. Much irresponsible comment has gone into connecting the environment with large numbers of cancer cases. It's not been proven. When a cold statistical eye is applied to what percentage of cancers are caused by the environment, it's something like three or four percent if we exclude smoking and lung cancer. It almost seems as if cancer is part of the human condition.

"It's probably true that everyone's body has cancer cells, or mutations that could be malignant, but mostly we deal with them. Sometimes we don't, so medical science must deal with *that*. We'll go on waging the war, losing some battles, but seeing tremendous victories too."

Chapter FIFTEEN 🌿

*T*his conviction of hope is one of the things that enables doctors like John Truman to stay so long in the demanding and sometimes distressing field of childhood cancer.

During the time that I was talking to the Mass. General families, I took a short winter trip to the Bahamas, and I had an experience there that made me painfully aware of the disappointments and the losses of anyone who works with very sick children.

Leaving Harbor Island to come home, we took the ferry to Eleuthera, then a taxi to the airport, which is a strip of concrete and a shed. As we sat on our bags outside, a cry was raised, "Is there a doctor here?"

I leaned across to look into the doorway of the shed. In a corner, a rising panic of women's voices: "Is there a doctor here? A nurse?"

My nursing career ended a long time ago. Taking a pulse and blood pressure is about my limit, but I felt my body get up and walk into the shed.

"I'm a nurse."

The crowd parted. Murmurs of "She's a nurse." Sighs and smiles, as if I were a savior. If they only knew.

No going back. In the corner, a very young woman was sobbing in the arms of another. A huge middle-aged woman held a swaddled baby on her broad lap. I lifted the shawl.

"It's dead," she said. It was black, but you could see that it was blue.

Three weeks before, I had taken a cardiopulmonary

resuscitation course at a fire station near home. It wasn't a very comprehensive course, compared to others I have taken since, but our jokey CPR instructor Lenny had padded it out with many oft-told anecdotes and finished by promising us that if we were lucky, someone would have a heart attack in the next few weeks, and we'd be there!

Point illustrated by the dog-eared story of the woman who stopped at a restaurant on her way home to celebrate her certificate for the CPR course, and the vegetable chef obligingly collapsed under the steam counter to give her the chance to save his life with the mouth-to-mouth resuscitation she had practiced on the hideous rubber dummy in the blue track suit.

With infants, you put your lips over the nose and mouth to breathe them and press the chest with only two fingertips rather than the heel of your hand. The baby felt rather cold, but the dramatic voice of Lenny was in my head: *You'll save a life. Don't stop doing it. Don't give up. If you're alone, go on doing it as long as you have the strength.*

The grandmother said from time to time, "It's no use. He's dead," but I kept on. I was sure I could perform a miracle. When I did not, it was more surprising than if I had.

"He die on the boat." The grandmother wrapped the baby up again and gave it to the women who were with the mother, and they took a taxi back to the ferry. They had been going to Nassau to see a heart specialist, since the baby was born with a defect and had almost died twice in its first three months of life.

"I'm sorry. The mother . . ."

"Don't worry." The grandmother had been unconcerned all along. "She got plenty more at home."

But not this one. I had touched many dead bodies in the hospital, laying them out at dawn before the day shift arrived to complain that we not only let livable people die, but expected someone else to do the dirty work. I had

never kissed a dead person. On the plane leaving the island, my mouth still wore the feel of that tight cold skin
on the tiny nose and obdurate lips that would not breathe
for me.

I was totally downcast. I had done it wrong. I had let
old Lenny down.

"Stick to your guns, fight to the last ditch," he had
commanded, using the battle terms against heart failure,
as they do in cancer. "Don't give up. Thirty minutes, an
hour, two hours. Fight to win."

I thought about Dr. Truman and Monica and Sue and
the young nurses with their sweet, serious faces, and how,
although most of their patients survive, they must lose the
fight sometimes, because their weapons are still not as
sophisticated as the enemy's.

I remembered Laura telling me about the time she took
Krissie back to the hospital with chicken pox, perilous to
a child on chemotherapy. She had left Krissie to go to the
admissions desk, and from there she watched Dr. Truman
walking slowly down the corridor. Two of his babies had
just died on the ward, and she saw him stop before he
opened the door of the room where Krissie waited and
take a deep breath and change his face.

"Not knowing what had happened, we needed all of him
for us, and he gave us what we needed."

Children's doctors who are afraid of death don't last long
in cancer units. To those who stay, death is an enemy not
to fear but to fight.

Many of the young doctors who come into the field of
childhood cancer stay only a few years. Those like John
Truman, who has been in this work for twenty years, have
to develop ways to protect themselves, if they are to remain useful.

You can love the children and the families as friends,
but you cannot become too close. First names quickly used

and dinner with the family can lead to getting emotionally burned out when the tragedies happen.

Burnout is a term that is sometimes used by people in the helping professions who have to leave and start doing something else. They are probably exhausted, but it can also be that although they are dedicated, they are not quite wise enough. They see burnout as something that happens to you with time, an inevitable result of giving a lot in your work to people in any kind of crisis. Actually burnout is something you do to yourself, and it is the result of not giving quite enough. The final gift, the ultimate caring wisdom is to preserve your own personal life and the inner core of your feelings, so that you can go on helping indefinitely.

It's vitally important to have other interests and a satisfying life away from your work. Kathy, who has nursed very sick children for fifteen years, grasps a lot of outdoor life for herself, walking in the woods and by the sea, camping with a good friend, finding a peace under the sky that helps her to make sense of things that go wrong.

"Sometimes I can't help taking things home, for instance, if I've been in on a meeting where Dr. Truman has had to tell a family that the cancer has come back. That's the worst time, especially if the child is still on chemotherapy. The best drugs have been used. There are others, but there is a lot less hope. I see the parents' faces, and I can't forget that. I've grown to love the child. My mind can't leave him in the hospital. I have to walk home fast, get angry, cry, get it off my chest to someone who'll understand and not say, 'You've got to get out of this work.'

"I've got to learn to lay it to rest. The children have helped me. They are all so strong, but gentle too. They've changed me. My vision of life is different. They want to be well *now,* and I've learned not to look too far ahead, but to live for the moment. Whatever it is, sad or joyful, I live it.

"Some nurses say that they can let go of the sad things, but I can't always. We're told we shouldn't get too involved with the patients, but how can you help it? If you lose a child, you have to somehow get yourself going again and go on, because there is a next one who needs you, and another, and another.

"And to see how they cope with their dying—they're like teachers. I love life and I don't ever want to die, but when I do, it will help me to have watched how these children do it. After José died . . . after he waited for me to come back to see him and then died, I had to stay away from being a primary nurse for children with cancer for a while. I needed to get myself replenished, so that I could be good for the next child."

Dr. Harmon, who treats most of the teenagers who come into Dr. Truman's clinic or who have started there as children and become teenagers, finds it hard not to get too close to them.

"I identify very strongly with teens and young adults. Younger patients are sometimes easier. You're dealing more with parents, who have a fair amount of emotional maturity. But a teenager who hasn't yet grown up and who doesn't have a strong parent can be a burden to my feelings. He may call me 'Hey, Dave,' but I feel I have to be his father."

David Harmon, young, fresh skinned, with bright brown eyes and the same air of experience in harmony with innocence as John Truman, has been seven years in oncology. Does he see himself going on year after year like Dr. Truman?

"I'm not sure I could do as much of what he does all the time. He has excellent outside interests, his family, music, birds, reading—dozens of things he loves and takes time for. I have a tendency to shut out everything but work and do more and more until I'm exhausted and on the verge of saying, 'The heck with it. This is too much. I can't do it any more.' John has a better sense of balance. If he needs it, he takes time off. I've got to learn to do that.

"I've got to learn to let someone else cover for me. That's

hard if you're emotionally involved with patients. You feel indispensable, and that's not good. I want to learn from John how to be so comfortable with what I know that I can teach it to someone else well enough to trust them.

"There's so much to do, so much pressure. There are days when I feel, 'If I see another sick teenager . . .' Days when I say, 'This is stupid. Why am I killing myself? There are plenty of other people who could do this.'

"I get over that nonsense by going to bed. I take some time out for myself. Even just taking my lunch outside on the lawn. Or I jog or run. Something physical usually works.

"I get support too. No one else could do this kind of work as a lone operation. The nurses have a group where they can talk and let go, and we have a group of adult oncologists who have lunch together every other week with a psychologist. In theory, it's to help us to recognize the psychological and emotional problems of our patients. In practice, it often turns into a therapy session for us, and it's a very big help. John doesn't have that, but he has Monica and Sue and Cindy and the other nurses who work here, and they make their own little support group."

"That's important to all of us," Monica says. "I can't really tell my husband if I'm upset, because it upsets him too much and he fills up with tears. But we all talk to each other here and help each other.

"I couldn't do this kind of work for another doctor. There's no one like this man. I couldn't work here if it wasn't for John."

Sue can talk to one special friend, but not to anyone else outside the hospital. She talks a lot with the parents and finds that as helpful as they do.

"We don't talk about the cancer all the time. We practice a sort of healthy denial. Their child has a potentially fatal disease. We all recognize that, so why not be optimistic?

"It is hard, though. Sometimes I come home and say, 'I can't do this any more.' Well, what else then? I've put years into this work. I know I do it well, and I can't imagine anything that would be more challenging.

"What else keeps me here? John Truman. And the children."

Dr. Truman loses about a dozen of his patients each year. The losses of a doctor in this field are actually no higher than in the practice of a general physician, but other physicians lose mostly middle-aged and old patients. These are children.

Children are not supposed to die. Doctors who have difficulty accepting death (and it's curious how many do, in a profession with such high-risk customers) may choose pediatrics for that reason, just as doctors who are what the nurses call "socially retarded" may choose to work only in emergency medicine, with one-time contacts and very little need, as they see it (no one asks the patients) for an exchange of common humanity.

It is just this exchange and recognition that is one of the resources of a doctor like John Truman. From the sum total of his families—the old hands he never forgets and the new ones in treatment now—he gets continued strength and fresh confirmation of his belief in the unlimited potential of the human spirit.

How do the parents conjure up this kind of strength and continue to work so devotedly through all the months and years of their child's illness and treatment?

How do they do it?

This is the kind of simple litany you hear from everyone:

"You do it because you have to."

"Things happen. You deal with them. You do what has to be done."

"How do you cope? You just do. What else?"

"Inch by inch. After Paul's relapse, Dr. Truman said, 'We're going to fight this. We're going to win.' So I was able to harness myself, and we went on. Inch by inch."

"Sometimes you're exhausted, and you say, 'I don't want to do any more.' So you look around to see who else is going to do it—you know, the three-hundred-and-sixty-degree look—and there's only you."

"After Katie was first in the hospital in Madrid, I said, 'I can't go through that again.' But she was admitted here, much worse, so I did. There's nothing else you can do." That is often the time a mother will cry, saying that. "Now I don't think about it. You don't look at yourself as if you were another person and wonder how. You just do it, day to day to day to day, a day at a time."

"My husband cried a lot at first, but I said to him, 'That's it, we'll have no more of *that* kind of stuff,' " Nancy told me in a rolling-up-sleeves voice. "All the time Leo was sick, we didn't talk much about it. We just went on and did it, because that was the only way we could cope. You gotta take pills, you gotta take pills. You're gonna throw up, you're gonna throw up."

But underneath Leo's mother's brave discourse was a strong current of emotion that surfaced here and there. A sad memory of Leo's two roommates at the hospital, who had died. Flashes of rage against a tactless doctor—"I could have killed him!"—and a woman overheard gossiping about Leo in a restaurant. "I could have killed her with my bare hands, right there at the table."

I was reminded of a recent television film about suicide among the young in which the parents of an only child who had recently killed himself sat stony-faced, talking matter-of-factly about his life and death.

"Those people were so cold," someone said. "No wonder he killed himself."

But it was really no wonder that they appeared like that. It was the only way they could face the camera.

"Life goes on," Elizabeth said after her three-year-old died. "After it happens, it's a crisis for a while, and then it becomes part of life. It's always there. You live with it. Some people were shocked because we went to a business reception two weeks after our son died. But why not? Life goes on.

"Other people think Luke has disappeared. To us, he hasn't. He's still with us, part of our family, and he still has a lot to give us. He went out of this life when he was too little to know much, but now he knows far more than we do."

It doesn't destroy you. It changes you, everyone says. They speak of being more independent, stronger, liking themselves better, understanding what matters in life.

"I don't worry anymore about ridiculous things. The people nothing ever happens to are the ones who worry. They carry on about a scratch on the car, or someone forgot their birthday. That's like a foreign language to me."

"When I've had a bad day and I'm screaming because the children are screaming, I remember that one of them might not be here, and I'm glad to hear him screaming."

"The future? It's about a month long. You live in the present—I mean, you really *live*. Every day matters. I mean—that's so obvious. I can't think why I was too stupid to see that before."

"I used to be so shy, sort of girlish, with my pretty baby and my husband taking care of me. Poor man, he's got this woman now that I've become, who can do anything, drive anywhere, talk to anyone, argue with doctors, break down doors to get what she wants."

"One thing I've learned from the people who helped me: If someone's in trouble, don't hesitate to barge in and say something—anything, never mind if you can't say it without crying. Share it. Bring love. The love that pours in is the saving grace of tragedy."

"If Jimmy hadn't been so sick, I might never have known what kind of person he really was. I would never have known this wonderful side to my son."

For his funeral service, Ann wrote, "He appreciated the little things that the rest of us take for granted and was filled with a great satisfaction with each accomplishment.

"He couldn't run much. He couldn't ride a bike fast. He couldn't throw a ball far, and many a time it was an effort for him just to walk, but he was the strongest boy I'll ever know. He pushed so hard and endured so much to try to be a part of life."

"I wouldn't want to change anything about what happened," Deborah said. "I've gained so much, and David hasn't lost anything, because he's strong and healthy now, and he doesn't remember much of what he went through. If John asks me to come and talk to new leukemia parents at the clinic, sometimes I take David, to show them that a child who's been as sick as theirs, or even sicker, now is cured, with no permanent damage.

"I'm no better or stronger than them, but I have something to offer, because I've been through it. I recognize all their emotions—the pain and anger and the resentment because it's so unfair. 'Why us? Why me?' I've found part of my own answer to those unfathomable questions by helping other people to keep their hope alive.

" 'How did you cope with it?' they ask.

" 'Same way you will. One day at a time. One hour at a time.' "

"They rise to meet the challenge," Dr. Truman observes.

The parents almost never fall apart. The mothers don't have nervous breakdowns, except in the fantasies of exhaustion, when anything seems better than having to go on. Then they have a bit of sleep and they do go on. They get on with it and do what has to be done and never in a complaining or self-pitying way.

"They don't make martyrs of themselves . . . ever. Whatever people may be like on the surface of their lives— selfish, crude, pretentious, insecure, trivial, stupid—the underlying truth is the nobility and wealth of goodness in each human spirit, which blossoms forth in time of adversity.

"I'm lucky," John Truman says. "In this job, I see people at the worst time of their lives, but I see them at their best."